D1134060

CLASSIC
FILM
SCRIPTS

# THE THREEPENNY OPERA
## Directed by *G.W. Pabst*
### Adapted from the musical by
### *B. Brecht*
### *K. Weill*

*Lorrimer Publishing*

All rights reserved including the right of
reproduction in whole or in part in any form
Original German language film entitled Die
Dreigroschenoper copyright 1931 by Nero
Films International and its predecessor
Nero Films A.G.

This edition of the screenplay copyright © 1984
by Lorrimer Publishing Limited
First printing 1984
Published by Lorrimer Publishing Incorporated
*Publisher and Editor:* Andrew Sinclair

ISBN Paper 0 85647 006 6

Distributed exclusively in the United States of America,
its territories, possessions, protectorates and places
mandated to it, the Philippines and the Dominion of
Canada by Frederick Ungar Publishing Company Incorporated,
36 Cooper Square, New York, N.Y. 10003.

*Distributed exclusively in the United Kingdom and
Commonwealth by Lorrimer (Sales) Limited.*

This book is sold subject to the condition that it shall not,
by way of trade or otherwise, be lent, re-sold, hired out, or
otherwise circulated without the publisher's prior consent in
any form of binding or cover other than that in which it is
published and without a similar condition including this
condition being imposed on the subsequent purchaser.

Inquiries should be addressed to Lorrimer
Publishing Limited, 16 Tite Street, London SW3 4HZ
*Cover design: Fred Price*

# CONTENTS

# The Threepenny Opera (1931)

From *Celluloid* by Paul Rotha (London, Longmans Green & Co., 1933).

The scenario for *Die Dreigroschenoper* is loosely adapted from a musical extravaganza of the same name by Brecht and Weill, which in turn is distantly based on Gay's "*The Beggar's Opera*". Not a great deal of Gay's eighteenth-century spirit remains, however, in this new version. . . . Instead of an eighteenth-century London, we have substituted a most delightful, fantastic underworld set in a district approximating to Soho in the 'nineties, which is close to a romantically conceived dockland, with gay-life cafés and the most naughty yet highly diverting houses of ill-repute.

Any reader familiar with Pabst's work will at once appreciate what admirable scope such an environment gives for his love of darkly-lit, macabre settings, and for curious twists of vice and virtue. It can well be imagined how he delights in showing the romantic philanderings of Mackie Messer, the new Macheath, who is the captain of the so-called gang of London Apaches, and how Pabst portrays for our joyous entertainment the scandalous exploits of this charming hero.

At the opening of the film, Mackie falls in love at first sight with Polly Peachum, the beautiful and spirited daughter of the King of the Beggars, and marries her out of hand at a sumptuous wedding feast staged by his gang out of stolen goods in Mackie's sinister underground headquarters. When the wedding night is over, Polly steals home and breaks the news to irate parents, who promptly declare that she must divorce her newly-wed husband. Polly, of course, refuses to permit this, and Peachum goes to his friend, the Prefect of the Police, who also happens to be a good friend of Mackie, and tries to arrange at once for the latter's arrest. Warned by Polly of his danger, Mackie prepares to escape, but falls in with some old flames from the neighbouring brothel. He escapes the arm of the law, however, through the aid of his late love, Jenny the Whore, only to be caught as he leaves the abode of yet another attractive *cocotte*. The business-like Polly, meanwhile, has taken charge of the gang and has decided to fly on a higher plane by running a bank. But her father, incensed because he has not been able to obtain justice, plans to upset the Coronation procession by organizing a parade of his beggar-legions to spite the Prefect of the Police. He learns too late of Polly's success as a business woman, and fails to stop the trooping army of beggars from breaking up the procession. Whilst this is taking place, the faithful Jenny contrives Mackie Messer's escape from prison, just as Polly is arranging to pay the ransom for his release. Learning of her success, Mackie returns to Polly's extended arms, and the film comes to a happy conclusion with the launching of a new firm with Mackie and Peachum as the directors. Borrowing from Gay's original, the picture is interrupted at regular intervals by a street singer, who gives a brief résumé of the action and explains for the benefit of the dense-minded why and wherefore the characters are behaving as they do. In all, an amusing piece of lighthearted nonsense strung together with a brilliant parade of wit and a multitude of intriguing situations.

Passing over for the moment the polish of the character-playing and the subtle handling of the incidents, I would comment principally on the architectural environment which Pabst and Andrei Andreiev have jointly contrived for this comedy of manners. Not solely on account of their individual merit as design do I draw attention to these sets, but because they are the envelope, as it were, of the film. Without the self-contained world that they create, a world of dark alleys, hanging rigging and twisting stairways, without their decorative yet realistic values, without the air of finality and completeness which they give, this film-operetta would not have been credible. It is partly by reason of the queer, fantastic atmosphere created in this dockside underworld that this film is lifted on to a plane by itself. This is due not only to the settings in themselves, but the very close relationship maintained between the players and their surroundings, which has come about because the director and the architect have to all intents and purposes worked with one mind. Each corner and each doorway is conceived in direct relationship to the action played within its limits. This factor, together with the co-operation of the camerawork, builds the film into a solid, well-informed unity.

Actual instances of such dovetailed workmanship are too numerous to be detailed in full, but I praise especially the set representing Mackie Messer's headquarters, a piece of creative set design which deserves to be put on record. Presumably situated beside the wharves, it is built on three levels, the roof reaching to a considerable height. From a door at the top, an incredibly steep and very long flight of narrow wooden steps descends to the middle level, from which the inimitable Mackie Messer dictates his questionable correspondence to his secretary, who is seated at least twenty feet below him on the lower level. What a delightful touch of humour is this! On all sides of the set rise up great barrels, ridiculous barrels of absurd height and girth, yet how admirably original. Mackie's dressing-room consists of smaller barrels placed slightly apart, behind each of which he vanishes in turn to complete his toilet. Outside there is a salubrious erection of piles and arches and small bridges, a perfect ideological world for the Apaches of London, hung about with slanting masts and drooping rigging. The most delightful part of it all is that when the gang emerge from their huge cellar by the door in the ceiling, they arrive on the normal level of the streets outside.

Quite different but equally amusing is the late-Victorian brothel, with its paper-patterned windows and antimacassars, its multitude of useless ornaments and its giant negress statues standing about the room. Every detail in these sets is placed there with a definite purpose — to create the mood for the scene. In the twisted streets, in the prison, in the angular office of Peachum, in the underground café, this same striving for atmosphere is apparent and is tremendously successful. No other films in the world can create such an architectural environment so well as those of Germany.

This intimacy between the director and the architect is not all. The camerawork and lighting also are closely related to the settings and the action. The remarkable photographic genius of Fritz Arno Wagner must be added to the creators of the environment. His lighting, camera set-ups and camera movements are worked out in careful relationship to the sets and the action. When the camera is in motion, the smoothly sliding pan glides from one figure to another across the set with a perfect respect for its material. Low-level or high-level, its set-up and path of direction is governed by the mood of the scene, which is also the mood created by the set. . . .

Moreover, especial reference should be made to the prevalence of moving camerawork in *Die Dreigroschenoper*. Since the introduction of the spoken word into film-making, there has been a growing tendency to decrease the number of direct cuts in a picture, partly because of the desire to minimise the amount of different camera set-ups and partly on account of the difficulties attendant on cutting and joining the sound strip. . . .

As far as *Die Dreigroschenoper* is concerned, the moving camera is noteworthy in that it is used not so much for economic reasons as for its assistance in establishing the relationship of the characters with their environment. Pabst is far too skilled in cinematic sense to allow mere convenience of camera mobility to interfere with his fine expression of mood. This film abounds with instances of his uncanny instinct for selection of camera angles, particularly when several characters are grouped together. In addition to which, he employs his favourite method of making every cut from one shot to another on a movement, so that the eye of the spectator is carried smoothly from image to image, aided by the sound. This style of cutting will be remembered in *Jeanne Ney* and in *Crisis*, both significant pictures in Pabst's career.

In each of his earlier films, it will be recalled that Pabst has displayed an interest in the mental and physical make-up of his feminine players, with the result that he has often brought to the screen women who have been unusually attractive in a bizarre, neurotic manner, very different from the brilliantly turned out, sophisticated but stereotyped women of American pictures, or the dreary young ladies favoured by British directors. Pabst is one of the few directors in the whole film business who has any understanding of women. Whatever part they are required to play, or whatever clothes they wear, the women in Pabst's films never fail to be interesting, and those in *The Threepenny Opera* prove no exception to the rule.

To instance a small detail of the picture, the chance meeting of Mackie Messer and the stray street-girl after the former has escaped from the brothel is one of the most amazingly well-handled incidents that I have ever seen on the screen. How it is contrived I do not pretend to know, but Pabst extracts the very last ounce of meaning out of the scene. The enticement of the woman and her physical magnetism are brought out in all their human strength despite the fact that she herself is far from being attractive in the ordinary sense of the word. Similarly, Messer's indifference gradually turning to fascination is remarkable. An effect of cynicism is not gained wholly by acting, but by Pabst's rendering of the scene, by his choice of angles and by his deep psychological understanding of the elements of the situation. The scene in itself is an admirable example of his close penetration into the depths of human behaviour, and the way in which he recreates an ordinary human experience on the screen. Further evidence of this extraordinary quality abounds in the film, as in the diverting women of the brothel, the scenes in the café, the wonderful reunion between Jenny the Whore and Mackie Messer, and the treatment of Polly throughout. To any close observer of Pabst's outlook, these are in direction tradition with certain scenes in *Pandora's Box, Jeanne Ney, Westfront 1918, Crisis* and *The Diary of a Lost Girl*. . . .

Under Pabst's direction all the cast of *Die Dreigroschenoper* play with an exquisite charm and purposeful deliberation of gesture to correspond with the fantasy of the plot. Rudolf Forster makes an engaging Mackie Messer in grey bowler-hat and canary-yellow gloves; Carola Neher is immensely attractive as Polly; Fritz Rasp and Valeska Gert, familiar to all followers of the German cinema, bring experience and humour to Mr and Mrs Peachum; whilst those who remember the genial Communist attaché in *Jeanne Ney* will delight once more in Vladimir Sokolov as Schmidt the Gaoler.

Good as the poised acting may be, it is the direction of this film that causes its cynical drollery and sinister melodrama to be so effective. It is the controlling, creative mentality of Pabst that combines the thrills of a crook drama with the light melodious atmosphere of an eighteenth-century operetta. Whilst the plot is essentially one of wit and humour, nevertheless we feel through it all a sense of drama. It is a supreme genius of cinematic art that can bring out the subtleties of the situations, envelop the whole delightful extravaganza in charm, and still preserve a touch of dramatic feeling. The direction of Pabst grows on one and becomes curiously fascinating. Like *City Lights, The Threepenny Opera* is at its best when seen for a second time.

*Extracts from an interview by Gideon Bachmann with Jean Oser, who worked with Pabst as editor on many of his films*

From *Cinemages 3: Six Talks on G. W. Pabst* (New York, the Group for Film Study Inc, 1955).

GB: You started working with Pabst on *Westfront*?
JO: Yes, I was working for " Tobis ", the company who owned the

patents on sound reproduction. That in itself is quite a story. Tobis had a monopoly on all sound film production in Germany because they had bought up all the Swiss, Danish and German patents. They were the only ones who could actually make sound films. You had to rent the sound crew and equipment from them. I was working for Tobis, and so when Pabst wanted to make a sound film he got the equipment from them and I became editor for him. . . .

. . . After *Westfront 18*, he went into *Dreigroschenoper*, which he did for Warner Brothers, but again Nebenzahl (owner of Nerofilm) was involved; it was a deal between Nebenzahl and Warner Brothers. *Dreigroschenoper* was a very hot property at the time: it had come out as a big theatrical hit; in fact it was almost phenomenal how much it influenced a complete generation.

GB: You mean the play. . . .

JO: Yes. When *Dreigroschenoper* came out, it formed the entire pre-Hitler generation until 1933; for about five years. It was not just a big success like, for example, " South Pacific " — not every young American girl today would like to act and look and talk like Nellie. When *Dreigroschenoper* came out, every girl in the country wanted to be like Mackie. Apparently, the ideal man was the pimp. Warner Brothers thought that this was a big hit and they bought the rights for *Dreigroschenoper* from Kurt Weill, who had written the music, and Bert Brecht, who had written the play.

GB: Did the actors from the play work in the film too, like Kurt Gerren and Lotte Lenya?

JO: Only Lenya, the rest were different. They had Rudolph Forster as Mackie Messer; Reinhold Schunzel, as Tiger Brown; and they had a very fine actress, Klabund's wife, Carola Neher, as Polly; Valeska Gert, as Mrs Peachum, and Fritz Rasp as Peachum. This film again was made in two versions, with different actors, for release at the same time in French-speaking and German-speaking countries. In the French version they had Albert Préjean as Mackie, and a young musical actress, quite well-known in France at the time: Florelle, as Polly. After the success of *Dreigroschenoper*, she became Number One star in France. Gaston Modot was in the French version as Peachum. The film was released in France as *L'Opéra de Quait' Sous*, and was a tremendous success. In Germany it was not such a success and it was attacked quite often by the critics.

GB: Tell me something about the production of *Dreigroschenoper*.

JO: When Pabst started this film it was immediately budgeted as a very big film, and he soon had trouble with Weill and Brecht.

GB: Why?

JO: Because Brecht had a different approach, and I must say in this case I agree with Brecht, because you don't make a million-dollar movie out of a story which should practically be shot in a backyard. The charm and the power of the theatrical production was in the fact that it was an opera performed by beggars, so that nothing cost anything. And now suddenly you see a thing which is photographed on the biggest set that had ever been made for a German movie up to that time. They built the complete harbor of London. Somehow it just didn't fit the story; it was too lavishly produced. I happened to see it again in France a few years after it was made, and by that time the print had become old and scratchy and somehow it had more reality for me then, than when it was new and shiny. I must say, though, that what Pabst himself told me about his difficulties with the authors, sounded quite different. I was the editor and was not in on the script conferences, so I don't know what actually happened, but he told me that Brecht and Weill wanted to make it even a bigger production than he wanted to. He said they wanted to have 5,000 people in the wedding scene and wanted to shoot it in the big Sports Palace in Berlin, which is something like Madison Square Garden, so I don't really know who was right. Anyway, there was fighting from beginning to end, and when the picture was ready, Kurt Weill went into the act too, and they sued Warner Brothers and Nerofilm for not having hollowed the music exactly. I remember that there was one trumpet fanfare when the beggars start their march which was not officially composed by Weill, and on the basis of that, Warner Brothers and Nerofilm lost the suit. In those days, there was an interesting state of affairs: whenever an artist sued a producer, the artist generally won. But in this case I don't really think it was justified. Brecht and Weill won the suit and got — I think — 50,000 marks, which at the time corresponded to $50,000, and also — which is very interesting — the right to re-do the film if they wanted to.

CREDITS:

| | |
|---|---|
| Script by | Leo Lania, Bela Balasz, Ladislaus Vajda |
| from the play by | Berthold Brecht |
| Music by | Kurt Weill |
| Directed by | G. W. Pabst |
| Producer | Seymour Nebenzahl |
| Production company | Warner Bros.-Tobis |
| Photography | Fritz Arno Wagner |
| Sets | Andrei Andreiev |
| Musical director | Theo Mackeben |
| Sound | Adolf Jansen |
| Editor | Hans Oser |
| First shown | Berlin, 19th February, 1931 |
| Length | 3,097 metres |

## CAST:

| | |
|---|---|
| Mackie Messer | Rudolf Forster |
| Polly | Carola Neher |
| Tiger Brown | Reinhold Schünzel |
| Peachum | Fritz Rasp |
| Mrs Peachum | Valeska Gert |
| Jenny | Lotte Lenya |
| The vicar | Hermann Thimig |
| The street-singer | Ernst Busch |
| Smith | Vladimir Sokolov |
| Mackie Messer's gang | Paul Kemp |
| | Gustav Püttjer |
| | Oscar Höcker |
| | Kraft Raschig |
| Filch | Herbert Grünbaum |

(The French version, which was shot concurrently with the German version, using the same sets, had the following leading actors: Albert Préjean (Mackie Messer), Florelle (Polly), Jack Henley (Tiger Brown), Gaston Modot (Peachum), Jane Marken (Mrs Peachum), Margo Lion (Jenny), Antonin Artaud, Vladimir Sokolov, Marcel Merminod.)

17

# THE THREEPENNY OPERA*

*Scene 1. A street in London.*

It is afternoon and the atmosphere is gloomy. A brick façade
. . . one side of the street is taken up with solid-looking houses,
warehouses, storage depots and old office buildings; we are to
assume that the way down to the docks and the river is on the
other side. The district is frequented by pallid-looking people
— typical members of the lower middle classes and dock-
workers on their way home. Some are lounging in doorways,
children are playing in the street, housewives are going home
laden with shopping-bags. The last notes of the overture are
heard as the sequence opens on a long shot of the street. Among
the passers-by are POLLY and MRS PEACHUM, shot unobtrusively from behind.

They are on their way home and the camera tracks behind them
as they walk past a house with its entrance right on the street
corner. An ornate signboard hanging over the doorway pro-
claims the name 'Highgate Marsh' and above that, on an iron
bracket, is the red lamp that glows day and night to light
people to brothels. At that moment the door opens and
MACKIE MESSER, whom we can see only from behind, appears
in the doorway with JENNY. The notes of the 'Tango Ballad'
can be heard from inside the house. The camera comes to a
standstill. POLLY and MRS PEACHUM walk out of the picture
without noticing MACKIE, who happens to catch sight of them
and hesitates, looking after them with interest.

We now see MACKIE from the side. In the twinkling of an
eye his expression changes: this bleary-eyed fellow, who's
obviously feeling rather morning-afterish, has visibly perked
up; he straightens his hat and takes a step to the side to get a
better look at the women. He pushes back JENNY as she tries

* The version presented here is taken from the original shooting script
for the film, a copy of which was kindly provided by the Munich Film
Archive. Major divergences from the final version of the film are indicated
in the notes at the end of the script, which also contain stills references.

to follow him and sets off in pursuit, accompanied by the camera. As he passes a ground-floor window of the house, a woman rapidly hands him out his cane;[1] he takes it mechanically, without looking at the woman, and continues on his way. The music gets softer. The scene is repeated at the next window, except that this time another woman holds out his gloves. MACKIE is still looking straight ahead and again takes the gloves with a mechanical movement; he sets off after POLLY, who has now disappeared, swinging his cane. The music stops. Close-up of MACKIE from in front. The camera keeps pace with him as he goes faster and faster, his cane tapping feverishly along. Behind him in the distance, JENNY and the other women watch him as he walks away.

Now we follow POLLY as seen by MACKIE, with part of her mother's arm hanging onto her. The camera tilts up from POLLY's feet to her bottom and stays there, tracking with her. MACKIE is seen in back view, with MRS PEACHUM and POLLY now further ahead. The two women turn into a side alley; behind them, only a few steps away, MACKIE quickly follows and turns the same corner.

*Scene 2. A small square.*
We follow MACKIE as he enters the square, in the middle of which a crowd of people can be seen grouped around a STREET-SINGER, who is hidden from view. A barrel-organ is playing the beginning of 'The Ballad of Mackie Messer'. MACKIE walks up to the bystanders and joins the crowd, looking for POLLY.[2]

Seen from behind, MACKIE stands on tiptoe, looking for POLLY over the heads of the people in front of him. A tall man with a shabby top hat is blocking his view, and MACKIE quietly flicks the hat to one side with his cane so that it slides down over the man's ear.

A closer shot from MACKIE's point of view. In the middle of his field of vision is the STREET-SINGER, who is singing and illustrating his words with a series of pictures. Beyond him, in the front row of the audience, is POLLY's face, which we, and MACKIE, now see indistinctly for the first time.

Close-up of the STREET-SINGER as he sings, turning from side to side with comic gestures and pointing to the different pictures with his stick; each of the crudely painted designs illustrates one of the verses. Next to him is a bare-footed girl playing the barrel organ. The ballad continues.

Shooting from where the SINGER is standing, the camera pans across the spectators. The man with the top hat listens open-mouthed and mechanically straightens his hat, so that MACKIE'S face disappears behind it. The pan continues as MACKIE moves in a wide semi-circle round the edge of the crowd so that he can stand beside POLLY. Among the audience we see a stout couple, a moustachioed petit-bourgeois with his plump wife, a servant girl with a soldier, who stands dumbly as if posing for a photograph, and two teenage girls sucking liquorice sticks. MACKIE has now come up behind POLLY; he pushes his way through to her and comes to a halt behind her and MRS PEACHUM as the first verse of the ballad ends.

Close-up of POLLY, seen from inside the circle of spectators. MACKIE'S face appears just behind hers as the second verse of the ballad is sung. Unnoticed by POLLY, MACKIE looks at her, fascinated, and pushes closer. We get the impression that he wants to touch her. POLLY starts and turns her head towards MACKIE. He looks up simultaneously and, laughing, sings the last line of the third verse with the STREET-SINGER: '. . . But evidence is rather thin . . .'

We cut to the STREET-SINGER with his pictures as he sings the fourth verse.[3]

MRS PEACHUM is seen from behind. She is bored and leaves her place, dragging POLLY with her. POLLY can't take her eyes off MACKIE, and draws him after her with a look. All three of them go out of shot as the fourth verse comes to an end.

Resume on the STREET-SINGER with his pictures; he begins the last verse.[4]

We now see the ring of spectators from where the STREET-SINGER is standing. The camera pans round, showing the reactions of the audience, then holds on the faces of the girls, who as the SINGER comes to the word 'raped' leave their liquorice sticks in their mouths in a thrill of voluptuous horror.[5]

*Scene 3. Outside the Cuttlefish Hotel.*

We are at the entrance to a tavern with a signboard depicting a huge cuttlefish hanging up over the door. MACKIE is seen coming up the street behind the two women, who are laughing.

MACKIE: *May I invite you ladies to step into the Cuttlefish Hotel with me?*

He gestures invitingly towards the tavern. POLLY is still gazing at him with an ecstatic expression on her face, but MRS PEACHUM gives him a knowing wink and leads the way down the steps, looking a bit prim but clearly flattered by the invitation. POLLY follows her and MACKIE brings up the rear. As the women go in through the door we hear music coming from inside. MACKIE pauses at the bottom of the stairs, turns and whistles.[6] A man rushes down the first few steps and MACKIE goes back up towards him.

Seen from above, MACKIE gives an order to WAT DREARY.

MACKIE: *Tonight at two o'clock. In the Duke of Devonshire's stables. Bring a vicar with you. Furniture and fittings, the lot. I'm getting married at ten past two.*

WAT is flabbergasted, but MACKIE has already gone back down the steps and into the inn.[7]

WAT climbs the steps. He pauses a moment, peering furtively round in all directions. Then JIMMY, who has been unobtrusively patrolling the area round the tavern entrance, walks up to him. They have a whispered conversation. JIMMY nods and goes down the steps into the inn, while WAT quickly makes himself scarce. Loud music can still be heard from inside.

*Scene 4. The Cuttlefish Hotel.*

It is a typical London pub, clearly frequented by sailors, judging by the model ships hanging from the ceiling and the stuffed fish in cases round the walls. The decor is plushy, vulgar and Victorian — elaborate upholstered furniture, lots of copper knock-knacks, a portrait of Queen Victoria very much in evidence. In the middle is a small dance floor. The bar takes up the whole of one side of the room; the music is supplied by a band. The camera pans right round the room to show the clientele dancing, drinking or just sitting. They are all members of the lower middle classes — barge-owners, captains of small boats, plus a few tarts and shady-looking

21

characters. WAT DREARY brushes past, giving whispered instructions. The drinks on sale are beer and whisky, and the dancing is highly decorous. The camera finally comes to rest on MACKIE and POLLY, who are dancing in the throng.[8] They gaze into each other's eyes, oblivious of what is going on around them. They continue dancing for a few seconds after all the other dancers have gone back to their seats, unaware that the music has stopped. MACKIE suddenly snaps out of it and they smile at each other as he leads the happy but dazed POLLY to the corner table where MRS PEACHUM is sitting. A waiter pours them out glasses of beer.[9]

In a close shot, POLLY settles herself slowly in her chair, her eyes still riveted on MACKIE, while MRS PEACHUM raises her glass to him. As MACKIE puts his glass to his lips, he notices someone at the bar. He slowly puts the glass down again and stares intently in that direction.

At the bar, CROOKFINGERED JACK is just raising his glass of whisky.[10] Feeling MACKIE's glance on him he instantly turns round and goes hesitantly over to MACKIE's table, his glass untouched. He is clearly embarrassed.

At MACKIE's table: JACK has come up and MACKIE whispers to him as he looks from MACKIE to the ladies. POLLY and MRS PEACHUM are sitting back in the corner out of earshot, busy with their beer.

MACKIE: *Two o'clock.*

JACK: *All right. We know all about it.*

MACKIE: *Make yourselves look spruce. Don't any of you come looking like that. After all, it's not just anybody who's getting married.*

The music begins again, gliding softly in a tango rhythm. MACKIE introduces JACK, who is trying to start on his drink, to the ladies.

MACKIE to MRS PEACHUM: *He's the best dancer in Soho.*

MRS PEACHUM is already getting to her feet; she takes JACK's arm as he looks first at MACKIE then at her, and reluctantly puts his glass down again. MACKIE has already danced off with POLLY. JACK throws one last glance at his beloved whisky as MRS PEACHUM nestles blissfully in his arms. They begin dancing near the table.[11]

22

The dancing couples are seen from the edge of the dance-floor, JACK and MRS PEACHUM and POLLY and MACKIE among them. MACKIE and POLLY move towards the camera and another couple, NED and his girl-friend, dance up to them. MACKIE speaks over POLLY's shoulder in a stage whisper as NED dances beside him.

MACKIE: *Tiger Brown must be invited to my wedding.*

NED still dancing: *The Chief of Police? He'll never come!*

MACKIE snapping at him imperiously: *Oh yes he will.* To POLLY, as they continue dancing: *I've arranged our wedding for two o'clock.*

POLLY: *Yes.*

The music continues as they dance off and the camera tracks in towards JACK and MRS PEACHUM. MRS PEACHUM has firmly taken possession of JACK, who is looking rather bashful.

POLLY and MACKIE dance past the bar, the camera panning with them from over the bar counter. MACKIE addresses MAT OF THE MINT.

MACKIE: *Don't forget the rugs. And a grandfather clock.*

He goes on dancing, looking at POLLY but speaking in such a way that MAT can't avoid hearing as well.

MACKIE: *A four-poster bed with a blue canopy.*

POLLY breathes her reply huskily, unable to tear her eyes from MACKIE's face.

POLLY: *Yes.*

The camera follows MACKIE as he goes on dancing.

MACKIE a shade more practical: *You've still got to have a wedding dress.*

POLLY whispering absent-mindedly: *Yes.*

MACKIE looks round; a lone dancer sidles up to him and he addresses him over his shoulder.

MACKIE: *Full bridal rig-out. Brocade.*[12]

He stops dancing and, with POLLY on his arm, disappears among the dancers.

MRS PEACHUM and JACK are seen dancing up to the table; JACK is clearly worn out. MRS PEACHUM sits down and pulls JACK down onto the bench beside her, in the corner. The camera tracks in on them. JACK is flushed, laughing unsteadily as he seizes his glass of whisky and makes to take a sip.

JACK: *I've always fancied the maturer type, ever since I was a kid.*

MRS PEACHUM moves very close to him, clutches his right hand so that he can't put the glass to his lips and gives an excited laugh.

MRS PEACHUM: *Yes.*

JACK has cooled down a bit now and doesn't really know what else to say; he struggles frantically to get at his whisky.

JACK: *You certainly know how to ginger a fellow up.*

MRS PEACHUM pushes JACK right into the corner, clutching his arm so violently that the whisky glass is in danger of falling.

MRS PEACHUM in great excitement: *Yes.*

JACK is virtually helpless. He's not really equal to the situation but he's doing his best to carry out MACKIE's orders, hesitating all the while between his thirst and his duty as a reluctant seducer.

JACK: *Wouldn't you like to . . .?*

MRS PEACHUM interrupts him, seizes hold of him and laughs immoderately.

MRS PEACHUM: *Yes.*

The glass of whisky finally drops from JACK's trembling hand and falls to the floor. There is the sound of breaking glass which continues into the next sequence. Fade out.


*Scene 5. The window of a ladies' dress shop.*

Fade in on the sound of breaking glass: the shop window has been shattered. In it there are various wax models arrayed in fashionable outfits; in the centre is a dummy wearing a wedding dress. Two men drag the dummy into the street, strip it and run off. The model is left standing in the street, stark naked. Fade out.


*Scene 6. A furniture warehouse on the first floor of a depart-ment store.*

Fade in; it is night. The large store room is crammed with beds, sofas, cupboards, tables etc. In the foreground are two elaborate double beds with canopies, one beside the other. In the darkness the STREET-SINGER's ballad is heard, being whistled from several different directions at once. Then we see the light of a strong torch as its owner gropes his way through the store room, leaping over various bits of furniture

24

and finally coming to a halt by the first of the four-posters. The whistling continues. Into the beam of the torch comes the figure of a man — MAT OF THE MINT. He sits on the bed to test the springs — the bed bounces violently. A voice comes out of the darkness:

VOICE: *No good, Too much bounce.*

The torchbeam and the camera move onto the next bed. MAT lies down on it and it holds firm. The voice comes out of the darkness again.

VOICE: *All right.*

The beam and the camera tilt up from the bed to the canopy and the voice speaks again in a matter-of-fact tone.

VOICE: *Blue. O.K. Go on.*

Now the other burglars come into the beam of light from all directions at once and before you can say Jack Robinson the canopy's being taken down and the bed's being dismantled while the burglars softly but nonchalantly sing the words of the ballad.

(*Scene 7 cut.*)

*Scene 8. Night scene by a small river.*
There is a full moon shining down on a gloomy-looking refuse dump, with assorted pieces of junk interspersed with stunted trees. A patch of grass is covered with bits of waste paper. The first notes of the 'Love Duet' are heard as the camera shows POLLY putting the finishing touches to her *toilette* behind a twisted and broken bit of fencing. MACKIE meanwhile walks up and down in front of the fence, humming to himself. POLLY pushes aside several planks in the fence and comes through wearing the stolen wedding dress. The couple wander off over the rubbish, oblivious to everything, clinging closely to each other. They halt by a broken cart and lean against it, gazing up at the moon; their figures throw long shadows on the ground. They sing the 'Love Duet' while the camera tilts up to the sky and back down to the rubbish on the ground. The shadows fade as the song comes to an end. Finally, the camera tilts up to the moon again just as it disappears behind a cloud. Fade out.

*Scene 9. A narrow, crooked street in the City of London.*
It is still night and the full moon emerges from behind the clouds and shines down over the rooftops. The camera tilts down from the moon onto the street. In the distance, a BEGGAR sits curled up beneath a lamp at the entrance to a drinking club, apparently asleep. Directly above him, on the other side of the street but nearer to the camera, JIMMY and WAT are climbing down a rope which is suspended from a window on the second floor. They are carrying a huge grandfather clock. JIMMY has now reached the bottom; WAT is still on the rope and hands JIMMY the clock, which he humps onto his back. At this very moment the clock begins to strike, emitting rumbling chimes accompanied by a carillon that shatters the silence of the night. The two burglars are appalled and very nearly drop the clock.

The BEGGAR is seen in close-up. He has a placard hanging on his chest announcing in capital letters that he is 'A DEAF MUTE FROM BIRTH'. But now he leaps up, startled out of his reverie by the clock's chiming.

BEGGAR bellowing: *Stop thief!*

The burglars, frightened out of their wits, glance towards the BEGGAR.

BEGGAR yelling, off: *Burglars!*

They drop the clock with a terrible crash and run for it.

We see them running away, pursued by the 'deaf-mute' BEGGAR, who is still shouting. People come rushing out from their homes. The thieves have now turned the corner and a POLICEMAN appears, coming in the other direction. He intercepts the BEGGAR as he rushes in pursuit.

The POLICEMAN seizes the BEGGAR, who is beside himself and shouting his head off. The local inhabitants gather round.

POLICEMAN haughtily, to the BEGGAR: *What are you yelling like that for? Who are you?*

BEGGAR pointing to his label in great indignation: *I'm the deaf-mute! Don't you know me, Officer? I saw it all. They'll have to give me the reward.*

POLICEMAN: *You'll get your reward, don't you worry! Come down to the station with me.*

Dissolve.

*Scene 10.* Tiger Brown's *office.*

The Policeman's last words mix into the roaring voice of Tiger Brown, who is seen standing behind his desk.

Tiger Brown: *The London Commissioner of Police will be hearing about you!*

He drums his fingers on the desk top in agitation. Before him stand the deaf-mute, who is under arrest and escorted by two policemen; behind them are a few more burly policemen, who stand like rocks as their chief's thundering washes over them. The camera tracks with Brown as he comes out from behind his desk and walks along the ranks of policemen, spitting out his words at each of them in turn. Meanwhile the Beggar follows the roaring Brown with his eyes, revolving on his own axis as the police chief passes behind him.

Tiger Brown: *It's not for nothing I'm called Tiger Brown. Ten break-ins a day and yet you lot still doze away while the bandits snatch the sheets from under your backsides!*[18]

During this lecture Brown has returned to his place behind the desk; he sinks down in utter exhaustion as he utters the last words. Then he catches sight of the deaf-mute, who is standing facing him.

Close-up of Brown's face past the Beggar's head. It darkens and he starts shouting again.

Tiger Brown: *What do you want now?*

The Beggar has resumed his 'deaf-mute' role. He pulls a little slate out of his pocket with a trembling hand and passes it across the desk to Brown, plus a slate pencil, so that he can write his question down. At the same time he points at the label hanging round his neck.

Brown, in close-up, looks momentarily perplexed; he glances from the label to the Beggar, then flies into a rage again, while the Beggar continues to point at his invalid's card as if to appease him. As Brown is looking helplessly from the Beggar to the policemen, the Policeman who arrested the Beggar bends down and tries to explain things to his chief.

Policeman: *... but the man definitely isn't ...*

Brown pulls himself together and roars at the Policeman.

Brown: *You just shut up!*

He leans over the table and silently, but with particularly clear lip-movements, tries to get his question across to the deaf-mute. The BEGGAR doesn't look happy at this and begins to gesticulate right under BROWN's nose, using sign-language. BROWN retreats in alarm and the BEGGAR snatches up his slate, scrawls his message on it at top speed and hands it to him. BROWN reads it.

From above, we see BROWN's hands holding the slate. The text reads: 'I saw it all. It was Mackie Messer's gang. Please give me the reward.' BROWN's hands fling the slate aside. He takes a writing pad, tears a sheet out of it and writes: 'Reward for giving information. One pound.' Just as he is signing it, another hand is thrust into the picture. It pushes a printed visiting card onto BROWN's desk, which carries the pencilled message 'From the Captain' in ill-formed capital letters. For a second BROWN's hands hold both bits of paper. Then the fist clutching the visiting card crashes down onto the desk and BROWN begins to roar again.

BROWN: *What sort of a filthy joke is this?*

The trembling BEGGAR, who is staring as if hypnotized at the voucher for his reward, surreptitiously tries to fish the bit of paper off the desk. The policemen standing near look tense and harassed. Next to BROWN stands the OFFICIAL who handed him the visiting card.

BROWN bellowing: *Do you expect me to sit here all night? Get out!*

OFFICIAL trying to pacify BROWN: *Very good, sir. I'll chuck the fellow out right away.*

He turns to go, but before he gets to the door BROWN yells after him.

BROWN: *Show him in!* To the policemen: *Get out the lot of you!*

Meanwhile the BEGGAR has finally managed to slide the voucher for his reward off the desk. He and the policemen all make for the door and try to crowd through, but become tangled with MAT OF THE MINT, who is on his way in. Eventually one of the policemen grabs MAT by the collar and shoves him into the room. The door bangs shut. MAT remains by the door, looking round with a nonchalance he does not entirely feel.

Close-up of MAT at the door; BROWN walks over to him, gives him a severe look and moves his head in an inquiring gesture.

28

MAT, wavering between confidence and fear, delivers his message.

MAT OF THE MINT: *The Captain requests . . . He's getting married at 2 a.m. . . . at the Duke of Devonshire's . . . Two o'clock sharp in the stables, the Captain said — right on the dot.* He adds in a confidential tone: *If not, there'll be a real to-do.*

BROWN is clearly struggling with a welter of conflicting emotions; he tries to say something but can't get a sufficient grip on himself; he grinds his teeth, then looks as if he's about to burst into tears. The camera tracks with him as he wanders round the room in a state of great agitation, kicking at the furniture; he pounces on a bundle of documents and flings it into a corner.

At the door, MAT is getting more and more alarmed as he watches BROWN's towering rage. Behind him the door is opened by the OFFICIAL, who has come to see what the noise is all about. He sticks his head round.

OFFICIAL: *Shall I chuck him out?*

BROWN comes rushing into shot, kicks the door shut in the OFFICIAL's face and turns towards MAT; he goes so close to him that he blocks our view of him completely, almost squashing him against the door. Breathing heavily, he seems about to launch into a violent outburst — but in the end takes a deep breath and speaks in a resigned tone.

TIGER BROWN: *I'll come.*

MAT backs hastily away through the door without taking his eyes off BROWN. BROWN stares after him, then lets his head drop. Fade out.

*Scene 11. On the rooftops of London.*
The full moon is shining down on the roofs of a large block of houses. In the distance we can hear the STREET-SINGER's ballad being whistled softly. Over the ridge of a roof appears first the back of a large armchair, then a larger part of it.

A pair of hands push the chair over the ridge onto the roof. The camera tracks with them and then we see NED swinging himself along the roof. The whistling gets louder. NED prances perilously along the roof-ridge like a tightrope-walker, balancing the armchair. Suddenly a shot is heard from the street.

29

NED ducks, using the chair as a shield.

Cut to the street as seen from the rooftop. Policemen are firing their revolvers, people are rushing up from all directions and in no time the street is swarming.

Beyond the figures of the shooting policemen, the tiny figure of NED wriggles his way across the rooftops in a series of leaps, brandishing the chair like a trophy. Shots and screams can be heard.

Close on NED as he makes his way acrobatically over the roof-tops, looking as if he is about to fall headlong at any moment. As the shots ring out he ducks behind the chair, using it as a shield. He is still whistling the ballad and stops only when a shot rings out, taking the tune up again immediately.

Close-up: a bullet rips a hole in the back of the chair.

NED takes a huge leap and disappears from sight. The notes of the ballad can be heard from somewhere far away.

*Scene 12. The main hall in the Duke of Somerset's castle.*

It is still night and there isn't much light, though the full moon is shining on the elaborate furnishings. A voice humming the ballad is carried over from the previous scene as the camera pans across the bound and gagged figures of the Duke's ser-vants, who are spaced out around the room — propped against the walls or slumped on the ground in a variety of painful-looking postures. They are all in their night attire. The camera moves to a huge piano in the far corner. Several of the bur-glars are struggling to cart it away. Two of the legs have already been unscrewed, and the third is removed as we watch. The burglars hum the ballad as they work. Then the four of them hoist the piano onto their shoulders; a fifth steps up to it and, just as they are about to set off with their load, plays on it the last two notes of the song.

*Scene 13. The outer wall of a large warehouse.*

It is still night. A large open window on the third floor is seen from below. An enormous bundle of rags is pushed out from inside the room onto the windowsill and plunges down to the ground. It is immediately followed by a second bundle, then a third; this last bundle falls open and a large runner winds down like a serpent from the third floor to the street. Two men run up and grab the end of the rug, stretching it taut.

The wall opposite, again shot from the street. Windows are flung open and figures in night attire gaze across at the warehouse.

We see the third floor of the warehouse again, from the first floor of the house opposite. The camera pans with the burglars as they swing themselves one at a time over the windowsill onto the carpet and then zoom down as if on a chute, bawling out the ballad as they do so.

*Scene 14. A telegraph cable, stretched high above the street.*
In the darkness a man works his way hand over hand along the cable, gripping a Venetian chandelier in his teeth. The glass tinkles in the rhythm of the ballad, taking up the song from the previous scene.

*Scene 15. A street with the window of a large delicatessen.*
It's midnight in Piccadilly; the traffic has stopped and the passers-by have gone home; a few night-birds are hurrying to their clubs and we can see prostitutes and men in evening dress. The shop-window is brightly-lit and full of enticing-looking delicacies. A van draws up unobtrusively, and the window is seen over its roof. Some men leap from the van and a stone is flung at the shop-window; there is an almighty crash and the sound of splintering glass.

Now seen from the van, the men start stripping the shop-window. Food and bottles fly in all directions; hams and tins of food are flung towards the van (i.e. towards the camera). Various passers-by rush up and a scuffle breaks out with the burglars using bottles, legs of ham etc, to beat their adversaries to the ground. Among the sounds of splintering, crashing, shrieking and the moans of the wounded can be heard the ballad which the burglars are bawling out at the tops of their voices like the ' Marseillaise '.

The burglars leap back into the van, which tears off, leaving behind it the empty window and, scattered on the pavement among the broken glass and debris, the victims of the Battle of Piccadilly. The camera moves rapidly in on the victims. The face of one of them is smeared with jam, another is hidden behind a layer of caviar; a third is choking on a chicken leg that's been rammed down his throat to act as a gag. And all over the victims flows a miniature river of champagne from the broken bottles. Rapid fade out.

*Scene 16.* TIGER BROWN'S *office.*
Fade in. All we can see is a file of papers on the desk, a hand holding it and a second hand leafing through the documents. The label on the front of the file reads 'Mackie Messer'. Sheet after sheet is flicked through and we scarcely have time to survey the long catalogue of crimes: two shopkeepers killed; breaking and entering; street hold-ups; murders; seduction; rape — and all these crimes were committed in a single month. Then come warrants for arrest, police orders, official minutes, and then suddenly in the middle of all these documents a large, yellowing photograph. The camera moves in and we see a picture of two solders riding on a gun-carriage; it moves in closer still and we recognize one of the faces as that of MACKIE, but the other one has been scratched out and cannot be identified. After a few moments one of the hands takes up a pen-knife and scrapes away at the face of the unrecognizable soldier, so energetically that it leaves a hole in the picture. Then the right hand snatches up the picture and thrusts it into a breast-pocket, as the camera tracks rapidly backwards to reveal TIGER BROWN. He pushes the photo down out of sight then rises from his chair, snatches up the bundle of documents and weighs it thoughtfully in his hand for a moment. He looks reflectively into the corner of the room, whence the camera now pans to show a large grate with a huge fire crackling away in it. BROWN reappears and the bundle of documents describes a broad arc as it flies through the air and into the fire.
BROWN's face is lit by the flickering flames as he watches the documents blazing away with a dreamy and contented look. It is the face of a man revelling in pleasant memories, happy in the knowledge that he has done his duty as a man and as an official. Slow fade-out.

*Scene 17. A large disused stable at the Duke of Devonshire's.*

Fade in. The door is flung open from the outside and in the moonlight we see the silhouettes of two of the burglars standing on the threshold; with revolvers and torches at the ready they jump down into the room.

FIRST BURGLAR yelling: *Hello, anyone there? Hands up if you are!*

SECOND BURGLAR after a short pause: *Is anyone there?*

FIRST BURGLAR: *Not a soul! We can celebrate our wedding here without any trouble.*

His companion turns towards the door and looks out into the street. A whistle signal is heard.

*Scene 18. Open country in front of the stables.*

They are long, barn-like buildings in the country on the outskirts of London and are surrounded by meadows and fields divided up by fences. Waggons laden with furniture are seen driving up to the gateway to the stables. The sound of wheels and the cracking of a whip echo through the silence of the night. The men jump out of the van and start unloading. Dissolve.

*Scene 19. A London street.*

Three waggons are driving rapidly past, one behind the other. Another two waggons emerge from a side street and join the procession. Dissolve.

*Scene 20. A main road.*

A long column of waggons is bowling along in the moonlight, joined at various intervals by other waggons pouring into the main road from various side roads. Soon the procession is heading rapidly towards its destination, the waggons travelling three abreast. Dissolve.

*Scene 21. Inside the Duke of Devonshire's stables.*

We look right through the stable to the open doors. There is a confused jumble of furniture, rugs, furnishings of one sort or another, and food. The stable is teeming with people feverishly arranging the furnishings, hanging curtains, fixing chandeliers to the ceiling or putting pieces of furniture in position, while more and more furniture is continually being carried through the gateway. There seems to be very little hope of ever bringing any order to this scene of chaos. The stable echoes with the sound of hammering, shouts, etc. Rapid dissolve . . .

The stable is now fully furnished and has been transformed into an ultra-posh reception room. The door is closed and there is not a sound to be heard . . . All by himself in the centre of the room stands the helpless figure of the VICAR, a worthy fellow in a black frock-coat, a sort of missionary. He looks fearfully round the room, his hands clutching convulsively at his prayer-book.

The camera pans right round the room, following his gaze. As we catch glimpses of the splendid furnishings the burglars emerge from all corners of the stable, from alcoves and from behind folding screens and curtains. They are all in evening dress but unfortunately their subsequent behaviour hardly matches the elegance of their attire. They all gravitate towards a large cheval-mirror in one corner of the room to put the finishing touches to their *toilette*. On the way they give the VICAR a few words of encouragement; he looks nervously from one to the other, uncertain how to take their advances. One of them is stuffing the odds and ends from the pocket of his old suit into his dinner-jacket and in the process brandishes his revolver in the VICAR's face.

FIRST BURGLAR amiably: *Won't be long now, Reverend, and it'll all go off with a bang.*

A second BURGLAR claps the VICAR on the back in a friendly fashion.

SECOND BURGLAR: *The Captain'll be right pleased, Reverend, it's the happiest day of his life . . .*

Another, beaming, points to the furnishings.

THIRD BURGLAR: *A really first-class job, eh Reverend? Take a look at the stuff. It's all top quality . . .*

The camera tracks with the last speaker as he goes up to the mirror, which takes up a whole corner of the stable. It's a cheval-mirror with side-pieces, stolen from a tailor's workshop. As the burglars throng around it, helping each other to tie their bow-ties, we can see them reflected over and over again, their reflections grotesquely distorted.

*Scene 22. Outside the stable.*

34

The furniture-vans have disappeared, the gateway is shut and everything looks peaceful, as if nothing had happened. An open landau drives up and comes to a halt. MACKIE helps POLLY out and presses a note into the COACHMAN's hand; the COACHMAN humbly thanks him and chases off lest the noble lord should repent of his generous tip. MACKIE offers his arm to POLLY and moves towards the door.

*Scene 23. Inside the stable.*
We see a table groaning under the weight of a wedding feast. Sofas, easy chairs, armchairs and even deckchairs are grouped round it, so that all the many guests can have somewhere to sit. Several of them are inspecting the table with a critical eye and tasting the different dishes. CROOKFINGERED JACK shoos them away from the table and pulls out his watch.
JACK solemnly: *Ten past two!*
As they all turn to look towards the door, JACK takes up a bottle of champagne and undoes the seal.

*Scene 24. Outside the stables.*
MACKIE, with POLLY on his arm, is about to ring the bell on the door. At that moment the champagne cork goes off with a loud report inside. MACKIE takes fright and draws his revolver. The door opens and we see into the stable, where the burglars are grouped in a semi-circle. They break into a resounding cheer as the orchestra plays a fanfare.

*Scene 25. Inside the stable.*
As the last two cheers ring out we move inside again. Seen past the assembled guests, the bride and bridegroom enter through the door. MACKIE takes no notice of the cheering and turns his attention exclusively to the furnishings. He walks towards a wall-cupboard next to the doorway.
MACKIE examines the cupboard critically, while POLLY stands at his side looking round her in fascination, but with apparent incomprehension.
MACKIE: *Trash!*
JACK comes into the picture and bows low.
JACK: *Congratulations! There were people on the first floor at 14*

*Ginger Street so we had to smoke them out first.*

The camera tracks with MACKIE and POLLY, leaving JACK behind. MACKIE stops in front of a sofa and examines it critically; just then ROBIN OF BAGSHOT comes up to him.

ROBIN: *Congratulations! A constable kicked the bucket down in the Strand.*

MACKIE continues his tour of inspection. When he gets to the piano WAT DREARY approaches.

WAT: *Congratulations! Only half an hour ago, ma'am, the piano belonged to the Duchess of Somerset.*

MACKIE: *A rosewood piano and a Renaissance sofa! It's inexcusable.*

He opens the piano, plays two notes with one finger, then lets out a yell of rage.

MACKIE: *It's out of tune!*

He slams the lid shut, and the camera tracks with him as he sets off rapidly towards the table. He is pulled up short by the splendid armchair, looks startled, bends over to get a better look, then glances up reproachfully. NED appears in the frame, an anxious expression on his face.

NED: *Congratulations.*

MACKIE motions scornfully to the chair with his cane.

Close-up: the tip of the cane digs into the bullet-torn fabric of the chair.

NED sounding distressed, off: *I did what I could but the whole of Scotland Yard had turned out. Congratulations.*

MACKIE shrugs his shoulders, speechless. He goes over to the banquet, notices something on the food and bends over to look more closely.

Close-up of a dish of egg-mayonnaise. There are splinters of glass in it; MACKIE picks one up between two fingers and raises it in the air.

We see MACKIE holding up the tiny splinter of glass; his expression is withering but he maintains a scornful silence. The burglars look very upset. JIMMY steps forward, removes the bit of glass from between MACKIE's fingers and tries to smooth things over.

JIMMY: *The eggs are from Selfridge's. There should have been a vat full of pâté foie gras as well, but ...*

MACKIE cutting in scornfully: *From Selfridge's eh? And what about the splinters?*

JIMMY: *They're from Selfridge's too. Fourteen people rather fell by the wayside, but I don't think it's anything serious. Congratulations.*

MACKIE looks past him, at a loss for words; his expression is one of real consternation. (Throughout this scene POLLY has been hanging onto his arm, uttering not a word but merely looking at him rapturously whenever he says something.)

MACKIE: *And the clock? There's no grandfather clock!*

JIMMY pacifying him: *It's sure to arrive sooner or later.*

MACKIE: *My wife is very upset. You've really let us down!*

The burglars, who are still standing round in a semi-circle, turn and point proudly to the back of the stable.

BURGLARS shouting: *Reverend!*

The VICAR is standing bewildered in a far corner of the room. He looks lost and helpless, but comes hesitantly forward in answer to their shouts. The bride and groom come into shot.

MACKIE: *This, Reverend, is Miss Peachum, who loves me so much that she has followed me and wishes to share the rest of my life.*

As he introduces POLLY, we cut to a close shot of the three of them. The VICAR bows low to POLLY, then leafs through his prayer-book and begins to read the marriage service. We hear MACKIE's and POLLY's responses.

The camera now pans over the faces of the listening burglars as they follow the ceremony; they look very moved and solemn. The ceremony ends and the VICAR quickly joins the couple's hands. The burglars hurry forward from all sides, thronging round MACKIE and POLLY, almost knocking over the VICAR in their haste. Finally, JACK thrusts the others aside and takes up his position before MACKIE.

JACK: *Please allow us, Captain, on this happiest day of your life, in the spring-time of your career, I mean to say at this turning point . . .*

MACKIE interrupts him because he has just noticed that the VICAR is taking advantage of the general excitement to slip past the guests and out through the door.

MACKIE: *Come, Reverend, won't you honour us with your presence on this special day?*

Close-up of the VICAR, who is already at the door.

VICAR: *Thank you, thank you, but I must hurry away to a christen-*

*ing.*

NED *off:* *We'll soon be needing you for one of those too!*

While he is speaking the VICAR makes good his escape. MACKIE reprimands NED.

MACKIE *severely: Shut your trap. We'll have none of your dirty jokes in the presence of a lady![14]*

The orchestra sounds a fanfare and the guests rush towards the banquet. They begin to eat and drink greedily, while the orchestra plays.

A series of quick close-ups shows the guests eating greedily, stuffing caviar into their mouths with their knives, dipping their fingers into the bowls, with gravy running down their chins etc. There is a chorus of lip-smacking and munching over the music.

MACKIE is seated beside POLLY, eating nothing and surveying the whole banquet disapprovingly.

MACKIE: *I didn't want to start on the eating yet. We could have done with a bit of entertainment before you all rush to the trough. Other people always manage something of the sort on days like this.[15]*

JACK: *Such as what?*

MACKIE: *Well, why not sing a song to brighten the day up a bit? Do you want it to be just the same old wretched, gloomy day as ever?*

POLLY looks round in surprise, then glances anxiously at MACKIE as he continues to stare grimly at the company.

POLLY: *Well, gentlemen, if none of you wants to perform, I'll do my best to sing a little something myself.*

Everyone cheers and the orchestra strikes up.

The table is hastily pulled away from in front of POLLY; the rest of the furniture is also shoved aside.

Dissolve to a high shot over the guests seated around the walls to the large empty space in the middle of the room, where POLLY stands alone, looking small and lost. The orchestra plays 'Pirate Jenny' and POLLY sings.[16] There is applause and laughter as she comes to the end of the song.

Suddenly ROBIN rushes in through the door, shouting over the applause:

ROBIN: *Hey, Captain! The rozzers! It's the Chief of Police himself.*

There is a deathly silence.

Shot from the door, the burglars all scuttle out of sight behind the furniture and screens. MACKIE remains standing beside POLLY, who looks round in consternation.

BROWN enters the stable and looks round. He is not in uniform. MACKIE goes over to him and shakes him by the hand.

MACKIE: *Hello Jack!*

BROWN: *Hello Mack! I haven't got much time so I'll have to be going shortly. I'm on night duty. Did it absolutely have to be someone else's stable? Yet another break-in!*

The camera tracks with MACKIE as he leads BROWN along by the arm.

MACKIE: *But Jack, it's so convenient. I'm so glad you've come to join in your old friend Mackie's wedding celebrations.*

They have now come up to where POLLY is standing.

MACKIE: *May I introduce my wife, née Peachum? Polly, this is Tiger Brown, London's Chief of Police, the pillar of the Old Bailey, isn't that right, old boy?*

Cut to a high spot of the men grouped round the walls. While MACKIE goes on speaking, the burglars come shyly and cautiously out from their hiding-places. MACKIE makes a sweeping gesture.

MACKIE: *My Polly, and my men!*

BROWN interrupting: *Don't forget I'm here in a private capacity, Mack!*

MACKIE: *So are we, so are we . . .*

As he goes on speaking, BROWN bows to POLLY, kisses her hand and talks to her in an undertone.

MACKIE: *Gentlemen, you see in your midst today a man who has been placed far above his fellow men by the king's inscrutable decree and yet has still remained my friend, through all life's trials and tribulations and so on.*

MACKIE puts an arm round BROWN.

MACKIE: *Do you remember, Jack, how we served side by side in the Army in India?*

While MACKIE is asking this question BROWN looks with interest at the rug on which he's standing. MACKIE has followed his gaze.

MACKIE aside: *Genuine Shiraz.*

39

BROWN: *From the Oriental Carpet Company.*

MACKIE: *Yes, that's where we always get them. You see, Jack, I had to have you here today; I hope it's not too awkward for you, in your position.*

BROWN: *You know very well I can't turn you down, Mack.*

He hands him the photograph from his pocket. MACKIE shows it to POLLY, looking happy and moved.

The photo, in close-up, is seen past MACKIE's and POLLY's heads.

CROOKFINGERED JACK now approaches the group with a huge camera, simulating an elegant walk.

JACK: *And now a nice big smile!*

He sets the camera up. BROWN rapidly shakes hands with MACKIE and POLLY and speaks in a horrified whisper.

BROWN: *I really must go . . .*

The camera tracks with him as he rushes over to the door. MACKIE hurries after him and asks:

MACKIE softly: *Have they got anything against me at Scotland Yard?*[17]

BROWN equally softly: *They haven't got the tiniest thing against you at Scotland Yard. I've seen to that. Good night.*

While this short dialogue is going on — BROWN is already moving out through the door as he says the last words — JACK's voice rings out.

JACK off: *And now for the big surprise!*

We see JACK as he pulls aside the curtain.

MACKIE off: *What's going on?*

Amid general oohs and aahs, JACK unveils the four-poster. MACKIE comes into shot with POLLY on his arm. MAT OF THE MINT steps up to the bed from the other side and points at the canopy.

MAT: *Sky blue.*

A VOICE off: *Now for the photograph.*

All the burglars converge on the bed, grouping themselves round POLLY and MACKIE for the photograph.

The group are seen past the photographer. Someone tries to push to the front.

TWO VOICES off: *Stop! We're here too!*

JIMMY and WAT DREARY rush breathlessly into shot, still wear-

40

ing their ragged clothing; they pose right in the front, next to
POLLY and MACKIE, thrusting the others aside.

MACKIE looks severe.

MACKIE: *What about the clock? Where's the grandfather clock?*
The two of them seem to shrink under his gaze, and slink away
to the side; the camera pans with them as the other burglars
push them further and further towards the end of the row.

VOICES off, from the other end of the row: *Are we still in the
picture?*
The guests all stand in fixed poses, seen past the PHOTOGRAPHER
again.

PHOTOGRAPHER: *Lights out!*
The lights go out; voices are heard in the darkness.

PHOTOGRAPHER: *Hold it!*

NED: *How marvellous! It's a shame the bride's parents aren't here.*

MACKIE severely: *And the grandfather clock.*
JIMMY replies soothingly from the end of the row.

JIMMY: *We'll get it here yet.*

PHOTOGRAPHER: *A nice smile, please.*
As the flash flares we see the middle part of the group, with
MACKIE and POLLY posing formally in the centre. As the flash
goes out, the picture fades.
During the fade we hear the voice of the STREET-SINGER, which
seems almost unnaturally loud. He calls out like a town crier.

STREET-SINGER off: *You have been watching the love and marriage
of Polly Peachum . . . And now I'm going to show you the strength
of the Beggar King!*
As he finishes his speech, we fade into the next scene.


*Scene 26. Outside a church.*
The façade of the church is seen from below, with a flight of
steps leading up to the doorway; the bells are ringing and the
sound of an organ can be heard from inside the church on this
grey morning. A pair of beggars are standing on the steps as
the members of the congregation, mostly women, walk past
them into the church. The church-goers are all coming from
the same direction, and none of them gives the beggars anything. One of the beggars is blind, the other lame, and they
are making a great show of their infirmities, in a particularly

41

blatant way.

Seen closer now, they hold a whispered consultation. The BLIND BEGGAR gives his colleague a stealthy wink as if to enquire why it should be that not a single charitable donation is finding its way into their outstretched hands today. They turn to the edge of the steps and peer in the direction from which the members of the congregation are coming.

From the beggars' point of view, the camera pans over the steps and the parapet until it comes to the street along which the church-goers are approaching. It finally holds on a third beggar in the distance, who has his back to us and is being given some money by a passer-by. A second passer-by follows suit.

The other two beggars exchange comments in a rapid whisper. Then, as if nothing had happened and they had given up hope of receiving any alms, they get ready to set off for home. The camera tracks with them as they grope their way slowly and carefully down the steps, the lame one leading the blind one, a pair of pathetic-looking wrecks.

Resume on the street leading to the church, where the third beggar — FILCH — can be seen. The other beggars, SAM and HONEY, stumble haltingly past. When they come up to FILCH, the blind beggar, still hanging onto the lame one's arm, walks straight into him, making him step backwards a few paces. The two of them push relentlessly forward, the lame beggar barring FILCH's path with a threatening gesture. FILCH is visibly alarmed and shrinks back step by step until all three of them have progressed as far as the nearest street-corner.

At this moment the lame one — SAM — leaps forward, so that FILCH finds himself surrounded. SAM seizes his crutch and brandishes it at FILCH like a cudgel, while HONEY lands him such a blow that he staggers back against the wall.

HONEY in a rapid whisper: *How come you're pestering the passers-by, you swine? Have you got a licence?*

FILCH trembling: *Please, gentlemen, I'm broke. It's the wages of sin . . .*

SAM dealing him another blow: *So this small fry comes here and think's he's only got to stick out his paws and he'll land himself a nice steak.*

FILCH is doing his best to stammer out an excuse.

FILCH: *The thing is, gentlemen, I've been unlucky ever since I was a kid. My mother was an alcoholic so I sank deeper and deeper into the mire of the big city. And now you see me . . .*

HONEY interrupts him and gives him another bang on the head with his crutch, so hard that the crutch breaks.

HONEY: *We see all right. And if you let yourself be seen again you'll get it in the neck.*

As HONEY speaks, FILCH sinks to the ground beneath the blows, trying desperately to protect his head. The two beggars stop hitting him and HONEY presses a card into his hand. FILCH takes it nervously. But then the beggars transform themselves back into helpless cripples with lightning speed and disappear round the corner.

FILCH, in close-up, picks himself up awkwardly. He's been so badly beaten up that he can scarcely stand. He looks in amazement at the card the beggars have pressed into his hand, turns it over and over and then reads it.

We see the card in FILCH's hand, which reads: ' Jonathan Jeremiah Peachum & Co. — The Beggar's Friend — Beggar's outfits and licences — 83 Shaftesbury Avenue.' Dissolve. (The sounds of the church-bells and the organ music that have been audible at intervals throughout this scene mix into the ' Morning Anthem ' which accompanies the following scenes.)

*Scene 27.* PEACHUM'S *shop.*
We see the large signboard outside the shop which reads: ' Give and thou shalt be given. Shut not your ears to misery.' Dissolve.

*Scene 28. Inside* PEACHUM'S *shop.*
There is a large office with cubicles for changing in, and in the centre stands a double desk at which PEACHUM is seated, totally absorbed in his huge ledgers. The place is full of crutches, invalid chairs and old clothes hanging up, as in a second-hand clothes shop. Placards inscribed with biblical sayings are very much in evidence. On one side of the desk there is a large chest with five wax dummies representing the basic types of human wretchedness and on the other side a

43

modern strong-box or safe. In the background we can see a wrought-iron staircase leading up to PEACHUM's apartment on the first floor. PEACHUM sings the 'Morning Anthem.'[18]

*Scene 29.* POLLY's *room.*
It is a typical teenage girl's room, in the kitsch style of the turn of the century, with little lace mats all over the place, photographs arranged in a fan on the wall, pious texts, a guardian angel above the bed and above that a canopy with stuffed white doves. The last lines of PEACHUM's 'Morning Anthem' can still be heard wafting up from the shop below. The sequence opens with a shot of MRS PEACHUM opening the door and entering the room.

The camera pans slowly round the room from the door, eventually holding on the bed. It clearly hasn't been slept in, since POLLY's night things are all still laid out ready for the night. MRS PEACHUM stands in the doorway, too startled to say anything; she nervously wrings her hands and looks helplessly round.

PEACHUM off: *Mrs Peachum!*

MRS PEACHUM takes fright. She runs over to the bed and hurriedly rumples it to make it look as if it's been slept in.

*Scene 30.* PEACHUM's *shop.*
PEACHUM is seen with the crumpled-looking figure of FILCH beside him, looking at a map of London.

PEACHUM sounding businesslike: *Anyone intending to practise the trade of the beggar in London needs a licence from Jonathan Jeremiah Peachum & Co.*

FILCH: *A few shillings stand between me and ruin . . . But with two shillings in hand . . .*

PEACHUM: *Twenty!*

FILCH looks unhappily round the shop and then points to a placard.

Close-up of the placard; it bears the text: 'Shut not your ears to misery!'

FILCH off: *Ten!*

PEACHUM points to another placard behind him.

The text reads: 'Give and thou shalt be given.'

PEACHUM off: *Twenty!*

PEACHUM brings the deal to a close.

PEACHUM: *And fifty per cent of your weekly takings!*

FILCH sounding downcast: *All right.*

He fumbles about with his money and counts it out onto the desk while PEACHUM opens a ledger.

PEACHUM: *Name?*

FILCH: *Charles Filch.*

PEACHUM writes it down.

PEACHUM at the top of his voice: *Mrs Peachum!*

We see the staircase, past PEACHUM and FILCH at the desk. MRS PEACHUM appears on the stairs; as she comes down a whining voice is heard from the doorway.

BEGGAR off: *Greetings and peace be with you!*

A BEGGAR with a wooden leg comes into shot and walks up to the desk to stand beside FILCH.

BEGGAR: *I must complain most vehemently. This stump is just no good.* He lays his wooden leg down on the desk. *It's a really shoddy piece of work and I'm not going to throw my money away on it.*

PEACHUM is furious and shoves both the BEGGAR and his wooden leg away from the desk.

PEACHUM: *Wait there!*

MRS PEACHUM finishes coming down the stairs and walks over to stand beside her husband at the desk. As she does so the doorbell jangles several times and we hear a rapid succession of greetings from the people who come in, such as ' Good day to you ' and ' Praise the Lord '.

We look past PEACHUM to FILCH and the BEGGAR with the wooden leg, who are still by the desk. HONEY and a fourth BEGGAR now join them. HONEY walks very warily over to the desk and hands his broken crutch over the top of it to PEACHUM. PEACHUM doesn't look up from his book.

PEACHUM snapping at HONEY: *Wait there!* To MRS PEACHUM, pointing towards FILCH: *Number 314, Baker Street District, outfit number C.*

MRS PEACHUM moves away, motioning FILCH to follow her. But FILCH has recognized HONEY and has been observing him in obvious fury for some time. HONEY has recognised him too, and as he makes to follow MRS PEACHUM, he grabs him by the sleeve.

HONEY to PEACHUM: *This witness here can confirm that it wasn't my fault that my crutch got broken.*

PEACHUM to HONEY growling: *Clause No. 12: The firm cannot be held responsible for damage to items of equipment.*

FILCH tries to tear himself away from HONEY's grasp, but HONEY won't let go and starts spluttering.

HONEY: *But . . . it wasn't my fault!*

PEACHUM: *Shut up!*

HONEY beside himself with fury: *He got his thrashing in accordance with the statutes . . . it was in the service of the Organisation . . . and now I've got to pay for a new crutch?!*

PEACHUM slams his fist down on the table-top.

PEACHUM to FILCH: *Go and get changed!* To HONEY: *Wait there!*

FILCH slips hurriedly out of shot. The fourth BEGGAR pushes his way forward to hand PEACHUM his membership card.[19]

FOURTH BEGGAR: *Here's my takings!*

He lays the card and the money down on the desk.

PEACHUM goes over to the safe, takes out a smaller cash-box and stows the money away in it. MRS PEACHUM is standing nearby, busy hunting among the clothes on hangers to find an outfit that will fit FILCH. FILCH watches her with interest, then takes a look round and walks over to the wax dummies to get a better look.

We see the dummies past FILCH. He stops in front of a dummy wearing a large label marked with the letter C and looks round enquiringly.

FILCH pointing to the dummy: *What's that?*

PEACHUM, who is now back at his desk, interrupts his work to look up.

PEACHUM to FILCH: *Those are the five basic types of misery most likely to touch the human heart. The sight of such wretchedness puts people in that unnatural frame of mind in which they are actually prepared to part with their money!*

MRS PEACHUM brings FILCH his ragged outfit on a coat-hanger.

MRS PEACHUM to FILCH: *Get undressed and put this on, but look after it.*

FILCH looks uncomprehendingly from the rags to the dummy labelled C and then to PEACHUM and MRS PEACHUM (the

Just at this moment the bandits disappear through the door, which bangs shut so that the bell jangles.

We see the beggars' hands, which are still above their heads, and beyond them the top of the staircase. PEACHUM now appears on the stairs, in a state of great agitation; MRS PEACHUM follows him. He stops short and leans over the bannisters, dumbfounded, looking at the beggars.

MRS PEACHUM weeping: *Oh my Gawd! Mackie Messer! Lord Jesus save us!*

PEACHUM hurries down the stairs and the camera moves down with him; when he gets to the bottom he starts bellowing at the beggars, who are still facing the door, motionless, hands above their heads.

PEACHUM: *What's the matter with you?*

The beggars come to and begin to explain confusedly.

THE BEGGARS simultaneously: *Robbery! Mackie Messer! The safe!*

The camera tracks with PEACHUM as he forces his way through the crowd of beggars. He stands stock still in front of the now-empty safe, at a loss for words. The beggars stick close behind him, whispering in an undertone.

FILCH, in close-up, emerges from the cubicle in his new outfit. He looks at himself despairingly, shaking his head; then he walks past the beggars, who have their backs to him and are still gazing at the safe, past PEACHUM, who is rummaging about inside it, and up to the mirror. He looks at his reflection. He is close to tears as he takes off his cap and holds it out as if he were begging. He seems to be going through a dress rehearsal for his new career.

FILCH: *My mother was a drunkard, my father a . . .*

The doorbell jangles and we hear the cheerful humming of a happy man.

Cut to show the DEAF-MUTE as he comes cheerfully into the shop. FILCH looks at him in amazement; some of the beggars turn round as he marches over to the desk, holding himself exaggeratedly erect. He salutes, then makes his triumphant announcement.

DEAF-MUTE triumphantly: *Mr Peachum, one pound for denouncing Mackie Messer! Here's your fifty per cent!*

PEACHUM, apparently seized by an attack of hysteria, pounces

49

on the DEAF-MUTE, who looks at him uncomprehendingly.

PEACHUM bawling: *Ten shillings! For a paltry ten shillings you've set the whole gang at my throat!* He turns to the other beggars. *Get out, the lot of you!*

FILCH and all the other beggars retreat nervously to the doorway in the face of PEACHUM's fury.

*Scene 31. The street outside PEACHUM's shop.*

In a shot towards the door of the shop, POLLY drives up in an open cab, wearing her wedding dress. She climbs out of the cab just as the beggars back hastily out of the shop, then walks up to the door.

As she goes to open the door, in a close shot, PEACHUM's face peers through the glass; he looks at his daughter with a mixture of bewilderment and fury. POLLY presses down the latch and then enters. The beggars gather curiously round the glass door and peer through into the room.

*Scene 32. Inside PEACHUM's shop.*

As the bell rings, we look in through the glass door from the beggars' point of view. POLLY is standing happily in the middle of the room, while MRS PEACHUM is tearing her hair and PEACHUM is waving both fists excitedly at POLLY. We get the impression of a heated scene, but we cannot hear what is being said until a shout comes from PEACHUM.

PEACHUM: *Thieves' slut!*

MRS PEACHUM sinks onto a chair in a dead faint. PEACHUM fetches a bottle of brandy to revive her and she eventually comes to. PEACHUM looks up, catches sight of the beggars the other side of the door and flies towards them in a fury.

Seen from inside, PEACHUM goes up to the door and angrily throws it open. The beggars take to their heels; he closes the door, turns and says heatedly:

PEACHUM: *If you were going to be so immoral as to get married at all, did it have to be a horse-thief and highwayman, of all people?*

MRS PEACHUM off: *First we deck her out with dresses and hats and gloves and parasols . . .*

Close-up of POLLY, who continues to smile happily as her parents shout at her. MRS PEACHUM continues:

50

MRS PEACHUM: . . . *and when she's cost as much as a ship in full rig, she throws herself onto the dungheap like a rotten cucumber.*
PEACHUM: *You'll get a divorce!*
POLLY: *But I love him!*
MRS PEACHUM: *I'll tan your backside.*
POLLY: *That won't do any good. My love's greater than any hiding!*
PEACHUM: *One more word and I'll box your ears for you!*
POLLY: *Love is the most important thing in the world!*

The opening bars of the song 'Barbara' are heard. POLLY skips up the stairs to her room while her parents gaze after her, speechless with fury.

*Scene 33.* POLLY's *room.*
POLLY comes in, walks over to the mirror and starts to undress, singing the first verse of 'Barbara' as she does so.
When she is down to her petticoat the camera moves with her to the sofa; she kneels down on it and sings the second verse as she examines the photographs, which are arranged in a fan shape above.
We see the photos in close-up, over POLLY's head. Then she stretches herself out on the sofa, puts her arms behind her head and sings the third verse. She lies there pensively for a moment, then suddenly leaps up decisively and starts to pack various odds and ends (keepsakes, trinkets etc) into a bag; she then throws dresses and blouses into a suitcase. The final notes of the song are heard.

*Scene 34.* PEACHUM's *shop.*
On the lowest landing of the staircase, we see the heads of POLLY's parents as they discuss the situation, whispering heatedly. A barrel organ is playing off.
PEACHUM: . . . *notify the Chief of Police. If only they can catch him.*
MRS PEACHUM: *You leave that to me.*

POLLY appears on the top landing. She is still in her petticoat and is clutching a dressing gown, a comb, a brush and a powder-puff. She listens to what is being said downstairs.
MRS PEACHUM: *He's sure to be hiding with his gang. If he's got a date with one of his girls in a couple of hours he'll be well and*

*truly sunk.*

The parents are seen from above, with POLLY listening to them in the foreground.

PEACHUM: *Before the week's out they'll be taking him to the gallows, just as he deserves. I'm going to the Chief of Police.*

MRS PEACHUM: *And I'm going to his whores in Turnbridge.*

The parents grab their hats and coats and dash off; the door slams.[21]

Close-up of POLLY's face from below; her expression is one of utter dismay and full of conflicting emotions. As if to herself, she begins to sing the first lines of the First Finale (' Is it a lot I'm asking?'), apparently trying to justify herself in her own eyes.

*Scene 35. The* STREET-SINGER *with little girl and woman.*

The location is indefinite. To the accompaniment of a barrel organ, the little girl takes up POLLY's words (' Is it a lot she's asking?' etc). This is followed by an abbreviated version of the First Finale. Fade out.

*Scene 36. A store-room in the Duke of Devonshire's stables.*

We are in a room partitioned off from the main stable, glimpses of which (the four-poster bed etc) can be seen behind a curtain. The room looks distinctly like an office, with bookshelves, a typewriter and a huge armchair, though the remainder of the furniture contrasts strangely with this office equipment. The shelves carry a card index and there are some fat ledgers lying on the table next to the typewriter. MACKIE is lolling back in the armchair, while CROOKFINGERED JACK is struggling painfully to master the typewriter, laboriously picking out the letters. We can hear the machine clattering away as MACKIE dictates.

MACKIE: *Item number 7: Only strong rooms are to be burgled, after Oak Street. Nothing but cash is to be taken. No securities.* In an aside to JACK: *We must stick to safe stuff. We won't have anything to do with stock-market fiddles.*

MACKIE is seen past JACK. He is leaning arrogantly back in his chair and issuing his orders like a general.

MACKIE: *Item number 8: Wat Dreary will merely be the lookout man.* To JACK: *He's an untrustworthy scoundrel, always putting money into his own pocket . . . No need to write that down.* He continues his dictation. *Jimmy No. 2 is in charge of the explosives squad.* To JACK: *If he gets done in it'll be no loss to us. He's not on a retainer any more.*

JACK is seen past MACKIE. He is laughing so much that he has to clutch his sides.

MACKIE barking at JACK: *Your retainer's no laughing matter, either.* He leafs through a notebook. *One, two, three, four, five gold watches — that's not much for a month's work, my friend!*

JACK chokes back his laughter, assumes a solemn and gloomy expression and looks submissively at MACKIE as he waits for him to continue dictating.

MACKIE dictates and JACK takes it down.

MACKIE: *Item number 9: The break-in must be effected by 8.30.* Aside: *That's when the big fireworks will be held as part of the Coronation celebrations. All the doormen and caretakers will be watching the display.*

JACK: *And all the nobs'll be roaring drunk.*

POLLY comes into the room looking very upset.

POLLY: *Mack! Mack! Don't be afraid!*

MACKIE: *What's up? What's the matter with you?*

POLLY comes right up to him and puts her arm imploringly round his shoulders.

POLLY: *You must disappear for a while, and fast! You must start packing straight away.*

MACKIE draws her to him.

MACKIE: *What nonsense! Come here, Polly . . .*

JACK discreetly withdraws, looking thoroughly put out.

Close shot of POLLY seated on MACKIE's lap.

POLLY very agitated, to MACKIE: *I'm so frightened, Mac. They kept talking about hanging.*

MACKIE annoyed: *I don't believe a word of it. They've got absolutely nothing on me at Scotland Yard.*

POLLY: *They may not have yesterday, but suddenly there's an awful lot against you today.*

MACKIE: *I can rely on Brown. He's my best friend.*

POLLY rapidly, the words tumbling out: *I went to see Brown. And so did my father. And they arranged it between them that they were* going to have you arrested. Brown stuck up for you but my father made some terrible threats and he gave in.

MACKIE losing his assurance, but still incredulous: *What sort of threats did Peachum make?*

POLLY: *I don't know. But Brown stopped me in the corridor and said he couldn't do any more for you now.*

She goes to embrace him, weeping as she does so.

POLLY: *Oh, Mack . . .*

MACKIE leaps up, suddenly transformed into a trembling heap of misery. The camera tracks back a little as he stares at POLLY wordlessly, like a ghost. POLLY is so alarmed by MACKIE's alarm that she too stands stock still and stares at him aghast. MACKIE is seen past POLLY as he suddenly bursts out:

MACKIE: *Your father . . .! That's all the thanks I get for marrying his daughter!*

POLLY looks at him wordlessly for a moment, then collapses sobbing into an armchair. MACKIE has suddenly got control of himself again. The camera tracks with him as he walks rapidly over to the curtain that separates the room from the stable and pulls it violently aside. JACK has been eavesdropping behind the curtain. He starts back.

MACKIE barking at JACK: *Come here, all of you!*

JACK turns and rushes off.

POLLY is seen in close-up with tears in her eyes. She looks up and her grief slowly gives way to total bewilderment. MACKIE comes back and walks thoughtfully past her, taking no notice of her. She gazes fixedly at him, her face a picture of conflicting emotions but chiefly full of admiration and devoted love.

The burglars step out from behind the curtain one at a time; despite their nonchalant air they are obviously feeling awkward. POLLY looks from them to MACKIE, amazed at first, then calmer. MACKIE stands in the middle of the room and announces.

MACKIE: *I am unfortunately compelled to embark on a little trip.*

The burglars exchange glances of amazement.

MAT grumbling: *What, just before the Coronation? The Coronation without you'll be like soup without a spoon.*

JIMMY 2: *And what about our big bank job? You don't get Corona-*

54

*tion jamborees every year! It's such a good opportunity . . .*

MACKIE *snarling at* JIMMY 2: *Shut your trap.*

In a closer shot, MACKIE walks over to POLLY, who looks at him with a mixture of amazement and love. He strikes a pose and announces:

MACKIE: *I'm handing over the running of the business to my wife while I'm away.*

POLLY involuntarily rises to her feet, still staring at MACKIE, clearly unable to grasp what he is saying but happy just to see him speak. The burglars give a suppressed titter. MACKIE flashes a look at them, then the camera tracks with him as he strides rapidly over to the burglars, who instinctively line up in a row. He paces along the row, looking at each one of them in turn; they each stand to attention.

Shot of the line-up of burglars. MACKIE has now got to the end of the row.

MACKIE *addressing the burglars: The national celebration . . . The Queen's Coronation . . . must be a matrix . . . I mean a turning point for our business.*

As he speaks the camera tracks in closer and closer to him.

MACKIE *continuing his address: Let's have no more of this petifogging rubbish! Highway robbery, pickpocketing and all that sort of stuff is a loathsome business . . . you still haven't brought the grandfather clock!*

He glances reprovingly at the other flank of the line-up.

The two burglars who attempted to steal the clock bow their heads in remorse, then camera pans across to POLLY, who is standing in front of the line-up but on the other flank from MACKIE. She still has eyes for him alone. Meanwhile MACKIE is still talking.

MACKIE: *With the money we have from the deposit bank — I mean the money that will be ours tomorrow, we must put our business on a new and broader footing.*

He is seen in close-up as he finishes his speech.

MACKIE: *Let's away from Soho! And into the City!*

The burglars cheer.

MACKIE: *You've got some very hard work ahead of you. From now on you take your orders from my wife.*

We see him walk quickly past the line-up to where POLLY is

standing; she moves forward to meet him. He gives her a quick pat, then, as she clings to him and makes as if to accompany him, he walks on, speaking to her over his shoulder.

MACKIE: *Farewell, my love. Keep your chin up and don't forget to wear make-up every day — that's very important, Polly!*

MACKIE and POLLY disappear behind the curtain. The line-up disperses. At first the burglars gaze blankly at each other for several seconds; then one of them gives a scornful laugh and the others join in, digging each other in the ribs as though to say ' A fine mess we're in now!'

*Scene 37. The doorway of the stables.*
POLLY and MACKIE stand in the open doorway outside, silhouetted against the street.

POLLY clinging on to MACKIE: *Oh, Mac! Don't tear my heart from my body! Stay with me!*

MACKIE: *I'm tearing my heart from my own body, since I must go away and nobody knows when I'll be back!*

POLLY: *Don't forget me, Mack, in those foreign cities!*

MACKIE: *Of course I shan't forget you, Polly. Give me a quick kiss.*

POLLY: *And Mack, promise me you won't ever look at other women? Don't go to Turnbridge, don't go with other women . . .!*

MACKIE: *But it's you I love, and you alone! At midnight I shall fetch my black horse from some stable or other and before you see the moon from your bedroom window I shall be riding over Highgate Marsh!*

POLLY weeping: *Farewell Mack!*

MACKIE: *Farewell Polly!*

He tears himself away from her and leaves.

MACKIE singing off: *Love endures or fades away, either here or elsewhere . . .*

The distant sound of bells can be heard.

POLLY helpless as a small child:

> *The Queen to London is wending her way*
> *Where shall we be on Coronation Day . . .?*

*Scene 38. The room partitioned off from the stables.*
The camera pans rapidly across the burglars who are lounging in groups around the room. Some are stretched out on the armchair, others on the table, CROOKFINGERED JACK is sitting

on a pile of books; they are all puffing away at cigarettes, spitting on the floor, passing a bottle round. When the cat's away . . .

POLLY off: *I am taking over the command!*

The camera pans back across the groups of burglars as they react to POLLY's surprising command. One of them, possibly JACK, stares at her, his jaw dropping, and hesitantly hides the bottle of brandy, from which he was about to take a swig, in his pocket. Another BURGLAR in the second group, who has greeted POLLY's words with loud laughter, grows suddenly solemn and rises hesitantly to his feet, clearly called to order by the look on POLLY's face. A third BURGLAR, looking sullen and unwilling, but not daring to offer any resistance, straightens up and takes a last drag on his cigarette before stuffing it in his pocket.

The camera tracks with POLLY as she steps forcefully up to one of the burglars and looks him up and down with a critical eye; he stands almost timidly before her, holding himself stiffly. She reviews the whole line-up in the same way, and all the gang instinctively line up one behind the other, all of them looking stiff and awkward.

We look along the whole line-up from the opposite flank to where POLLY is standing. The burglars have dressed ranks as though they were on the parade-ground.

POLLY addressing the assembled ranks: *Now boys! I think our Captain can leave with an easy mind. We'll pull it off all right without him. Right boys?*

As she is speaking the camera tracks in towards her and holds when it comes to MAT. The others have been exchanging puzzled glances during POLLY's pep-talk, but MAT is still grumbling.

MAT OF THE MINT: *I haven't really got anything to say, but I don't know whether a woman, at a time like this . . .*

POLLY walks quickly up to him.

MAT weakening somewhat: *I didn't mean anything personal, ma'am.*

POLLY snapping at MAT: *You've certainly started off well, you swine! Of course you didn't mean anything personal, or these gentlemen would have shut your filthy trap for you. Right gentlemen?*[22]

The line-up is seen past POLLY. She looks up and down the row and they clap and cheer. JACK takes a pace forward.

JACK like a soldier: *You just give us your orders, ma'am, while your husband's away. Pay-day Thursdays, ma'am.*

POLLY: *Thursdays, boys. Dis-miss!*

The burglars slink quickly away behind the curtain.

POLLY calling after them: *Crookfingered Jack!*

JACK has got as far as the curtain but now turns and walks back. POLLY points silently to the typewriter.

Seen in close-up, he seats himself at the typewriter; POLLY comes into shot, reads through the last lines on the sheet that is still in the machine, then settles down in the armchair in exactly the same posture as MACKIE earlier on. She continues the dictation from where he left off.

POLLY: *Item number 10 . . .*

Just as she is about to begin she stops short and the camera tracks in towards her.

POLLY repeating dreamily: *Item number 10 . . .*

The camera closes in on her face. Dissolve.


*Scene 39. A vision of an imaginary marsh.*

Dramatic music. The vision opens with a long shot of an eerie marsh landscape, beneath a stormy night-time sky with tattered clouds. A lone horseman appears in the distance.

MACKIE is struggling against the rigours of the storm and the marsh, into which his horse is sinking. A peal of thunder is heard, and a dazzling flash of lightning lights up the sky, forming the words 'Highgate Marsh' in fiery letters. Dissolve.


*Scene 40. The entrance of the 'Highgate Marsh'.*

Close-up of the signboard of the brothel, with the words 'Highgate Marsh' inscribed in an ornate script. A thunderclap is heard. The camera tilts down to the street entrance as MACKIE marches blithely in through the door, whistling a little song and swinging his cane. He slams the door shut with a thunderous noise.


*Scene 41. The salon of the 'Highgate Marsh'.*

The room is furnished with tawdry elegance, full of plush

upholstery, mirrors, gilded furniture, little mats everywhere, little cupids, the whole atmosphere very bourgeois. The salon, which in the evening serves a large and bustling clientele with the aid of a piano and an upholstered sofa, is now, at five o'clock in the afternoon, being used as an ordinary living-room. An ironing board is laid across the backs of two armchairs; there is underwear lying on the piano; girls sloppily dressed in negligees are sewing and reading the papers at the same time. The sequence opens on a close-up of a pair of woman's hands laying out a pack of cards. At the same time a woman's voice is heard reading, stumbling over the words like a child.

WOMAN'S VOICE off: *Two shopkeepers killed, thirty burglaries, twenty-three hold-ups, eighteen cases of arson, seven premeditated murders . . .*

SECOND VOICE off, cutting in: *He's certainly managed to get together a tidy list, has Mackie Messer . . .*

As she utters MACKIE's name, the hands deal the last card — the knave of hearts.

FIRST VOICE off: *And in Winchester he seduced a pair of sisters, both minors.*

JENNY'S VOICE off: *I bet they weren't as minor as all that!*

In the middle of this sentence, the camera tracks back to reveal JENNY with her cards, then pulls back further to show us a GIRL READING THE PAPER perched on a stool nearby; beside her is a GIRL IRONING. A FOURTH GIRL is lying face downwards on a sofa reading an illustrated paper.

FOURTH GIRL interrupting the dialogue: *Look, girls, isn't this beautiful!*

The GIRL IRONING comes over to the sofa, the iron still in her hand, and so do two of the other tarts; they all peer over the recumbent girl at the magazine, while JENNY remains totally absorbed in her cards.

The cover of the magazine is seen over the heads of the girls. It depicts the Queen and the caption reads: 'The Queen's Coronation robe'.

JENNY pensively, off: *He's not coming back.*

The camera swings round to focus on JENNY, who is looking at her cards, lost in thought.

MACKIE off, from the door: *My coffee!*

JENNY jumps up, flabbergasted, and looks over to the door. The camera swings over from her to MACKIE, who has just come in, and tracks with him as he walks serenely across the salon, hangs his hat on the hat-stand and finally, crossing his legs, settles himself with great nonchalance into an armchair in the middle of the room.

MACKIE: *What's happened to my coffee?*

He looks round with a superior air.

The girls stare fixedly at MACKIE, looking as if they've seen a ghost. The GIRL READING THE PAPER is holding out the sheet from which she has been reading out the long list of MACKIE'S crimes.

GIRL READING THE PAPER stuttering: *Here's the warrant for your arrest . . .*

We see her hand holding out the page of the newspaper with MACKIE beyond. He pulls another paper out of his pocket, a bored expression on his face.

MACKIE: *I know. This is my usual Thursday visit. I really can't let such trifles upset my routine.*

He tosses the paper disdainfully onto the table.


*Scene 42. Part of a corridor with doors, in the brothel.*

Shot of a door in the corridor. BETTY (the tart who was reading the paper) flings it open. Inside the room a half-naked girl is standing in front of a mirror making herself up. As if announcing some unheard-of sensation, BETTY whispers:

BETTY: *Mack's here!*


*Scene 43. The brothel kitchen.*

The water for the coffee is boiling over on the stove, while a dirty little MAID of about fifteen sits huddled on a bench crying her eyes out; she has a well-thumbed novel on her lap. The door is flung open.

BROTHEL MADAME off, from the doorway: *Coffee for Mackie!*

The MADAME comes into the shot, rushes over to the stove and grabs the kettle.

MADAME snarling at the MAID: *What are you howling for? Nothing'll happen to him!*

The MAID is absorbed in her reverie and her voice is choked

with tears, while more tears fall onto her book.

MAID: '. . . It looked as if Count Botho would never see the golden-haired Else again . . .'

A VOICE off, from the corridor: Jenny . . .! Then more softly: Jenny!

Scene 44. The door of the salon from the corridor.
The door is opened from inside and JENNY comes out into the corridor. Piano music issues from the salon.

JENNY annoyed: Coming . . .!
We see part of the salon through the door, past JENNY's head. She shuts the door and walks out of the shot.

Scene 45. The salon.
The camera tracks with the MADAME as she carries a large tray bearing the coffee-pot, cups and a large cake over to the big oval table which is being rapidly laid by two of the girls. They unload the tray and the other girls come over and gather round the table. MACKIE is seated on the sofa in the centre. Everyone has been eagerly awaiting the coffee.

Scene 46. A dark corner in the corridor leading to the stairs.
MRS PEACHUM is on the stairs and JENNY is two steps above her, both of them seen from above. MRS PEACHUM is saying something eagerly and secretively and JENNY listens in fascination.

JENNY's face is seen past MRS PEACHUM, from below. Behind JENNY the first door in the corridor opens; a girl's head appears in the shaft of light coming from inside and she cocks her head to listen. MRS PEACHUM draws JENNY closer to her, whispers to her and then takes a banknote out of her handbag and presses it into JENNY's hand. JENNY stuffs it into the top of her stocking, with a swift but sure movement.

Scene 47. The salon.
Shot of the table with the coffee things, the door of the salon beyond. The scene is a real middle-class idyll with the table laid for coffee, the MADAME cutting slices of cake and everyone eating with great enjoyment. MACKIE is saying something as he raises his cup to his lips with his left hand and puts his right

arm round the girl sitting next to him.

MACKIE: *That's a nice bit of underwear!*

The girl laughs.

THE MADAME judiciously: *From the cradle to the grave underwear comes first!*

While these last words are being spoken JENNY appears and walks slowly over to the table; she sits down on a chair beside MACKIE but he takes no notice of her and continues to concentrate on his neighbour on the other side. JENNY helps herself to coffee.

JENNY casually, as she starts to eat: *Congratulations on your wedding, Mack!*

MACKIE, struck by her tone, hesitates; he stops flirting with the other girl, though he leaves his arm round her, and turns slowly towards JENNY. The girls all watch JENNY and MACKIE, surprised and interested.

Close shot of the two of them.

MACKIE: *Jealous, are you?*

He tries to draw JENNY towards him, realizing that she is angry and trying to calm her down.

MACKIE: *I'm married to you too, you know!*

JENNY pushes his arm away and retreats into her chair.

JENNY: *Yes — and to all of them.*

She points to the other girls, who laugh loudly. MACKIE looks down at her, thinking that she's in a very hostile mood today. Then he suddenly grabs at her brutally as if to say 'Stop playing the fool' and with a sure touch pulls the money out of the top of her stocking.

MACKIE surprised and approving: *Ten pounds — good girl!*

He pockets the money as he says this, then lets go of the other girl and draws JENNY close to him; she is so stunned at having lost her money that for a moment she forgets her hostility, but when he gives her a kiss she tries to ward him off. He takes a last sip from his cup, stuffs the last few crumbs of cake into his mouth and stands up. The camera tracks back.

MACKIE: *Now I must be going.*

JENNY, who is holding his left hand, suddenly looks at it and says:

JENNY: *Mack, when the bells of Westminster ring out for the Coro-*

*nation you'll have a bad time.*

The other girls draw closer, looking interested. They bend low over MACKIE's hand, their heads close to JENNY's. MACKIE looks nonchalant at first, then suddenly becomes interested.[23]

MACKIE looking at JENNY: *Just tell me the good part, please, nothing unpleasant.*

A GIRL: *Yes, Jenny, read his hand, you're first rate at that!*

ANOTHER GIRL: *What can you see then?*

JENNY: *I see a confining darkness without much light. And then I can see a capital C, which stands for a woman's cunning . . . Then . . .*

MACKIE is fascinated; he sits down again slowly and pushes the women aside.

MACKIE: *Stop! I'd like to hear a bit more about the confining darkness and the cunning. What's the name of this cunning woman, for instance?*

JENNY: *All I can see is that it begins with a J.*

MACKIE: *Then it's wrong. It begins with a P.* He stands up. *Goodbye!*

One of the girls brings him his hat and his sword-stick. JENNY is still clinging onto his hand, so MACKIE caresses her and strokes her hair.

MACKIE: *No, it doesn't begin with a J, Jenny! You've always been true to me . . .*

He turns to face the other girls as he pulls JENNY to her feet and hugs her tightly; she looks up at him; her face is full of conflicting emotions but her love for MACKIE and his fascination for her gradually get the upper hand.

MACKIE to the assembled girls: *And even though I'm Mackie Messer today, and my luck has turned, I shall never forget the companion of my darker days: Jenny, who was my favourite of all the girls!*

He begins to sing the 'Tango Ballad', holding JENNY close to him. When he gets to the end of the first verse, JENNY seems to snap out of her reverie. She notices the banknote in MACKIE's waistcoat and shakes off this indulgent mood. The camera tracks with her as she goes slowly over to the window, leans against window sill and starts singing the second verse.

A high shot past JENNY's head framed in the window to the street below, where MRS PEACHUM and two policemen are standing. While JENNY continues the second verse she makes an unobtrusive signal to the group in the street.

JENNY walks over to MACKIE as she sings the last words of the ballad; she puts her arms round him and they start dancing to the refrain. The camera tracks with them as JENNY gradually leads MACKIE over to the door, which slowly opens a crack. JENNY looks over MACKIE's shoulder and as the pair of them get close to the door we can see the figure of a man outside. MACKIE has his back to the door and is dancing happily.

The dancing couple are seen from outside the room. Several policemen are lurking in the corridor and a detective is waiting in the half-open doorway. In the background we can see the girls congregated round the table; they are gazing anxiously at the door.

Shot of a group of the girls. One of them has her hands to her open mouth as though she is about to scream, while another tries to signal to MACKIE.

JENNY and MACKIE dancing. MACKIE can't see either the door or the girl's warning signal because JENNY is dancing him right up to the door, keeping him with his back to it. At this moment SMITH springs forward and lays his hand on MACKIE's shoulder. He swivels round, startled. SMITH grabs his hands and goes to put handcuffs on him. MACKIE deals a blow at his chest, draws his knife out of his stick and escapes backwards to the window.

The policemen come tearing through the door. One of them raises his revolver but SMITH knocks his arm down.

MACKIE, having swung himself onto the window-sill, starts to slide down the drainpipe and disappears from view.

JENNY rushes over to the window and leans out.

*Scene 48. The street outside the brothel.*

The camera follows MACKIE as he slides down the drainpipe to the street. As he reaches the bottom the policemen who have been lying in wait for him grab him from behind and clap handcuffs on him. MACKIE is under arrest. MRS PEACHUM, who is standing nearby, gives a scornful laugh. MACKIE, having regained his composure, asks her politely:

MACKIE: *How is your husband?*

The policemen drag him off. Mrs Peachum follows at a distance, but turns round again to signal to Jenny. The camera tilts up to Jenny, who at that moment turns away from the window.

*Scene 49. Inside the salon.*
The girls are standing roughly in a circle, watching Jenny at the window. She has just turned back into the room and is clearly very disturbed, but has got herself well under control and looks serious, lost in thought. The tension is broken when one of the girls walks over to Jenny and spits contemptuously on the floor in front of her. Jenny does not react; with an angry and defiant expression she walks past the girl who has spat at her and through the circle formed by the other girls. They make way for her, staring in bewilderment as she continues over to the table where the playing cards are still laid out, and sits down.
Seen in close-up, she starts dealing the cards. The camera closes on the cards (as at the beginning of Scene 41).
Jenny murmuring to herself: *I wonder if they'll hang him?*
The grid pattern in which the cards are arranged dissolves into the prison bars in the next scene.

*Scene 50. A prison in the Old Bailey.*
The prison cells are more like cages on either side of a series of corridors; they are separated from each other by lateral corridors. The cells are in darkness but all the corridors are harshly lit from above. Most of the cells are occupied by prisoners. The sequence opens with a shot of Mackie's cell. First of all we see nothing but the bars, then Mackie emerges from the background and steps up to the bars. Brown approaches the cage from the outside. He seems very agitated and addresses Mackie in an anxious and imploring tone.
Brown: *It wasn't me: I did everything I . . .*
Brown is seen in back view, with Mackie on the other side of the bars. Mackie is gazing at Brown with a scornful and crushing look on his face. Brown is almost in tears.
Brown: *Don't look at me like that, Mack . . . I can't stand it:*
We see his face from the other side of the bars, past Mackie.

BROWN is thoroughly agitated. He presses his face, which is running with sweat, against the bars and is clearly on the verge of tears.

BROWN: *Your silence is awful: Say something, Mack! Say something to your poor old Jack!*

He virtually collapses and turns away from the bars, his hands to his face.

He staggers down the corridor between the cells, a broken man.

BROWN mumbling to himself: *He didn't even deign to speak to me!* As he stumbles past the cells the prisoners inside gaze after him. SMITH comes past and looks him up and down, shaking his head, then walks on to visit MACKIE.

Inside MACKIE's cell: SMITH opens the door and walks in, handcuffs at the ready. MACKIE looks at him enquiringly.

SMITH: *What's bitten the Chief?*

MACKIE: *It's a good thing I didn't shout at him. I just gave him a look and he wept bitterly. A little trick I got out of the Bible.*

While he is speaking SMITH has been putting the handcuffs on him. MACKIE inspects them critically.

MACKIE: *These must be the very heaviest you've got, Mr Jailer! With your permission I should like to put in a request for a more comfortable pair.*

SMITH: *But we've got them at all prices here, Captain. It all depends on how much you want to fork out.*

MACKIE: *How much does it cost not to have any at all?*

SMITH: *Ten pounds.*

MACKIE rummages in his waistcoat pocket to find JENNY's ten-pound note and presses it into SMITH's hand. SMITH promptly removes the handcuffs and backs away to the door, bowing obsequiously. MACKIE stands at the bars to watch him leave and begins to sing a shortened version of the 'Ballad of Gracious Living'.

*Scene 51. The entrance to the cells.*
We see a massive iron door with bars, set in a wall; it has a judas window which opens as LUCY, muffled up and wearing a veil, comes up and knocks shyly on the door. A vague outline of a warder's head appears framed in the judas.

WARDER: *Who goes there?*
LUCY: *Is my father still here?*
The door opens and the WARDER appears.
WARDER: *The Chief of Police has already left.*
LUCY: *Let me through!*
WARDER saluting LUCY: *Certainly, Miss Brown!*


*Scene 52. The prison in the Old Bailey.*
Shot of the corridor past MACKIE as he stands at the bars of his cell. LUCY is coming along the corridor, looking timidly about her as she does so. MACKIE clasps his hands together.
MACKIE: *The slut! That's all I needed. Now I'll have a fine time up to the execution!*
MACKIE turns away, pulls his collar up and his hat down to hide his face, then stands there with his back turned. LUCY comes rapidly up to the bars, reaches through and pulls at MACKIE's coat-tails.
LUCY: *You dirty swine! How can you look me in the face after all there's been between us!*
MACKIE turns to LUCY with a look of great surprise.
MACKIE: *Lucy?!*
We see the two of them, separated by the bars.
MACKIE trying to calm LUCY down: *Have you no heart, seeing your husband like this?*
LUCY: *My husband! You monster! I suppose you think I didn't know anything about your goings-on with Miss Peachum!*
A loud altercation can be heard coming from the entrance to the cells and POLLY's voice wafts towards us, the words tumbling over each other.
POLLY off: *. . . my husband! . . .*
Close-up of LUCY, with MACKIE in front of her.
LUCY taking no notice of the uproar: *I could scratch your eyes out! You're married to her, aren't you, you beast?*
MACKIE, one ear on the shindig outside, tries nervously to calm her down.
MACKIE: *Married! That's a good one! I visit this house regularly, I chat to her, I give her a peck on the cheek now and then, and now the old bag's rushing around shouting from the rooftops that we're married!*

67

POLLY off, but coming closer: *Where's my husband?*

She rushes into shot, not even noticing LUCY in her excitement, since she has eyes only for MACKIE.

POLLY clinging onto the bars: *Oh Mack, you told me you wouldn't go to those women ever again! Just think what your Polly's suffering to see you like this!*

LUCY scornfully: *The slut!*

POLLY noticing LUCY for the first time: *What's all this, Mack? Who on earth is this? Please tell her I'm your wife!* As MACKIE tries to pull her back her tone becomes more insistent. *Aren't I your wife?*

LUCY: *You dirty swine! Do you mean to say you've got two wives, you monster?*

POLLY speaking at the same time as LUCY: *Aren't I your wife?*

MACKIE trying to address them both at once: *If only you'd both shut your traps for two minutes I could explain everything.*

MACKIE is seen past the two women. POLLY and LUCY turn on each other and he tries unsuccessfully to separate them through the bars as they virtually tear each other's hair out. They begin to sing the 'Jealousy Duet'.

Shot of the corridor past the two women. As they sing the last lines of the duet we see MRS PEACHUM in the distance. She is arguing violently but inaudibly with SMITH, hurrying towards us as she does so. As the last words of the song die away we hear part of MRS PEACHUM's outburst.

MRS PEACHUM: *My son-in-law . . . I must see him!*

As she speaks she thrusts SMITH aside and storms towards the cell like an avenging fury, then lets fly at POLLY.

MRS PEACHUM: *You filthy little slut! Come home at once!*

POLLY: *Let me stay here mama, please, it's very important!*

MRS PEACHUM giving POLLY a box on the ears: *Oh yes? Well, that's important too! Quick march! When your fellow's hanged you can hang yourself with him!*

She drags POLLY away, while the girl yells and tries to resist her.

LUCY scornfully watches the pair of them leave, while MACKIE stands aloof. He gives LUCY a calculating look, then reaches through the bars and strokes her arm in a sort of caress, which makes her turn to him in surprise.

MACKIE: *You see how right I was? Is that how people treat their*

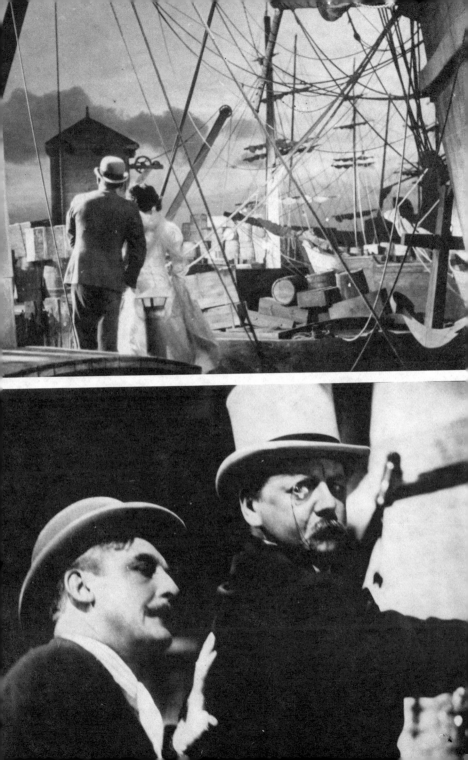

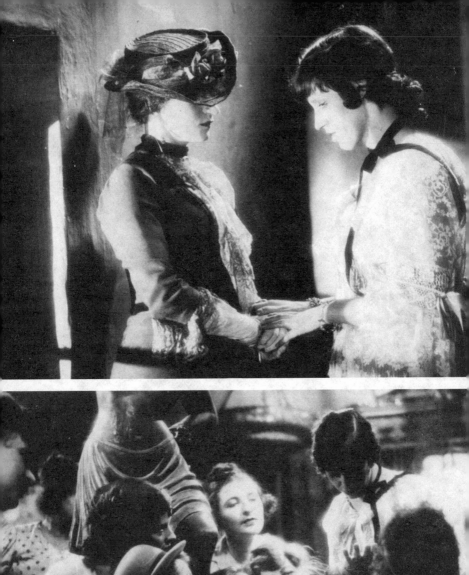

*son-in-law? Do you believe me now when I say there's no truth in it?*

LUCY is convinced. She caresses him through the bars, an expression of utter devotion on her face.

LUCY: *How happy I am to hear you saying that from the bottom of your heart! I love you so much that I'd almost rather see you on the gallows than in someone's else's arms!*

MACKIE urgently: *Lucy, I'd love to owe my life to you!*

LUCY: *It's wonderful the way you say that. Say it again.*

Seen past MACKIE, SMITH approaches along the corridor carrying MACKIE'S dinner. MACKIE notices SMITH and his voice becomes excited.

MACKIE whispering to LUCY: *Lucy, I'd love to owe my life to you!*

SMITH comes up to them and greets LUCY, beaming with pleasure.

SMITH: *Excuse me — may I serve the dinner?*

He walks along the cell towards the door; the lock clicks, while LUCY nods to MACKIE and then says something to him in a whisper.

Shot of the open door, past MACKIE. SMITH has come into the cell and is setting out the meal. Then we hear a cry from LUCY, as if she's about to faint. SMITH rushes out, leaving the door open.

LUCY is clinging to the bars as she swoons in a mock faint; SMITH comes into shot and catches her; He can't take his eyes off her, but she turns her head away and winks in the direction of the cell.

Seen from her point of view, MACKIE slinks over to the door and out of the cell.

LUCY, still pretending to be in a dead faint, is weighing SMITH down so heavily that he looks round despairingly for help, not knowing what to do; on the one hand he would like to summon help, but on the other hand he's thoroughly enjoying the situation.

In another cell, a prisoner sits gazing up in amazement at the wall above. The camera tilts up past him to show MACKIE decamping through a trap door high up in the wall. The prisoner follows his movements in great excitement.

Cut back to SMITH as he notices that the cell is empty. He

makes as if to abandon Lucy and goes to put his whistle to his lips so as to sound the alarm. But Lucy opens her arms wide and pulls him towards her, and he forgets Mackie and the need to sound the alarm in the face of this outburst of passion.

*Scene 53. The roof of the prison.*
Mackie saunters along the ridge of the roof and looks down.

*Scene 54. The prison yard.*
Seen from the roof, the prisoners are walking round the yard in a circle.

*Scene 55. The prison roof.*
It is now evening. Mackie, having seen the prisoners, turns to the other side of the roof, and skips over towards the fire escape.
Seen in close-up, Mackie prepares to climb down the fire-escape.

*Scene 56. The prison yard.*
In a corner of the yard, a couple of steps lead up to a side-entrance. The prisoners are still circling round the yard, and as the camera holds on the steps and the entrance it intersects a segment of the moving procession. Mrs Peachum and Polly are standing on the steps, framed in the doorway. Polly is fighting tooth and nail to get away.
Polly weeping and shouting at the same time: *Mackie! Mackie!*
Mrs Peachum struggles to pull Polly after her. As the prisoners come into the shot, they turn their heads to look at this scene, a mixture of boredom, sadness and indifference on their faces, but then calmly continue their circular walk.

*Scene 57. The fire-escape on the outer wall of the prison.*
Mackie climbs down with effortless ease and the camera tilts with him until he reaches the bottom. As soon as his feet touch the ground he glances round in all directions, then stops short.
Wide shot past Mackie of Suky, who is just turning the

corner some distance away.

MACKIE, in close-up, dusts himself down feverishly, pulls his gloves out of his pocket, puts them on and then sets off behind SUKY.

*Scene 58. The Old Bailey prison, MACKIE's cell.*
LUCY is still locked in SMITH's arms. He is quite oblivious to everything else as he abandons himself to her kisses.
MACKIE's cell is surrounded by corridors on three sides. The scene with SMITH and LUCY takes place in front of the cell, while the door through which MACKIE escaped is on the right hand side. It is along this right-hand corridor that BROWN now approaches, seen from behind.
Shot of BROWN past SMITH and LUCY as he comes along the corridor, then notices the open door and stops dead.
We see BROWN from inside the cell as he comes in through the door. His initial amazement gives way to joyous surprise and then to sheer delight as he satisfies himself that the cell is empty. Then his glance rests on the corridor in front of the cell and his face takes on an expression of bewilderment. The camera shoots past him on the embracing couple.
BROWN at the top of his voice: *Lucy!*
LUCY releasing SMITH: *Papa!*
SMITH has come to his senses and starts blowing his whistle like a man possessed. LUCY clutches onto the bars and speaks exultantly to her father, who is inside the cell, at the bars.
LUCY to BROWN: *I've freed him!*
Policemen rush along the corridors from every side.

*Scene 59. In the street.*
POLLY is being dragged along, weeping, by her mother; she has virtually given up trying to resist, but wails continually:
POLLY: *My husband! My poor husband!*

*Scene 60. A narrow alleyway.*
SUKY is seen from the front, with MACKIE in pursuit a few paces behind. The camera tracks ahead of them.
Now the camera tracks behind SUKY, from MACKIE's point of view. It tilts up from her feet to her bottom, lingers there a

moment, then tilts on up to her head. She turns her head and smiles, then slows down.

Resume on SUKY from in front as MACKIE catches her up and takes her arm. They walk away like a pair of lovers.

*Scene 61. The Old Bailey prison, MACKIE's cell.*

The policemen are standing round outside MACKIE's cell, seen from inside past BROWN, who has sunk exhausted onto the plank-bed. Also in the shot are LUCY, who is leaning against the bars, smiling, and SMITH, who is totally bewildered. Two policemen appear with PEACHUM.

ONE OF THE POLICEMEN: *Here's the Chief of Police.*

We see PEACHUM in the doorway of the cell, with BROWN in the foreground.

PEACHUM quite taken aback: *Oh! I suppose the other gentleman's gone for a stroll?*

BROWN sits on the plank-bed, struggling to hide his embarrassment. PEACHUM, in the foreground, looks at him spitefully.

BROWN: *Mr Peachum, I am quite beside myself.*

PEACHUM: *I come in here to visit a criminal and who do I find? London's Chief of Police!*

BROWN springing indignantly to his feet: *Damn it! I can't help it if the fellow gets away. The police can't do a thing!*

PEACHUM in a threatening tone: *I see. The police can't do anything, do you say? Hmmm . . .*

Close-up of PEACHUM past BROWN as he continues, with an increasingly triumphant expression:

PEACHUM: *. . . I'm curious to know what the police will do when the brillance of tomorrow's Coronation celebrations is marred by a march-past of a thousand or so beggars!*

BROWN: *What's all this?*

PEACHUM triumphantly: *Do you really think it'll look good if a few hundred crippled and mutilated people have to be struck down during the Coronation festivities?*

The two of them in close-up.

PEACHUM: *It would look bad. It's a disgusting sight, enough to make you sick.*

BROWN in a voice like thunder: *That's a threat! It's sheer blackmail! Policemen!*

The policemen stand stiffly to attention.

POLICEMEN in chorus: *Yessir!*

BROWN to PEACHUM: *Now you'll find out all about the Chief of Police's iron hand! It's not for nothing they call me Tiger Brown!* To the policemen: *Lock him up!*

Two policemen walk over and clap handcuffs on the totally bewildered PEACHUM. BROWN leaves the cell with the policemen.

BROWN to LUCY: *Come here, my girl.*

The door of the cell clangs shut. PEACHUM stands at the bars watching BROWN and LUCY as they go out of sight, the policemen marching behind them.

PEACHUM in a threatening tone: *You'll be browned off good and proper tomorrow, Mr Brown!*

Fade out.


*Scene 62. The* STREET-SINGER *with a small girl and a woman.* Fade in to the STREET-SINGER singing a shortened version of the ' Second Threepenny Finale ' accompanied by the barrel-organ. There is no indication of where the scene is taking place. Fade out.


*Scene 63. A corner of the stables* (MACKIE's ' *office* ').

POLLY is seated at the desk, while the burglars are lounging about in the foreground, some of them standing, some sitting down. A babble of voices can be heard. Then POLLY stands up and raps on the table with her pencil. Silence.

POLLY: *Let's away from the seedy streets of Soho and into the elegance of the City! My dear husband — I mean our illustrious chief — hit the nail right on the head when he said that! And now that he has once again escaped from prison and must lie hidden in unknown cities, he can rest assured that we'll pull off this bank business properly. Right, boys? We'll do a first-rate job, so that we can put our business on a broader basis at last!*

Cheers from the burglars. POLLY sits down.

Shot of the burglars past POLLY as she turns her attention to the accounts.

POLLY: *And now for the accounts.*

As the burglars don't stir, but just glance at each other eloquently, she looks up.

POLLY: *It's Thursday today, gentlemen.* She looks at the account book. *Crookfingered Jack!*

JACK steps reluctantly forward, assuming a troubled expression.

JACK: *Times are bad, ma'am! One silver watch.*

He lays it on the table and POLLY makes an entry in the book.

POLLY: *One silver watch.*

Some of the burglars titter. POLLY glances suspiciously round the circle and the titters die away.

POLLY reading from the book: *Mat of the Mint!*

MAT comes forward.

MAT: *It's been a very bad week, ma'am. One purse, contents five shillings and sevenpence.*

POLLY again writes it down, while the burglars burst out laughing.

POLLY: *Five shillings and sevenpence.*

She looks up very suspiciously and uncertainly; the laughter fades to a suppressed titter, which continues when she calls the next man forward.

POLLY: *Robin of Bagshot!*

He steps forward, looking very contrite.

We see ROBIN standing in front of the desk and POLLY behind it, with CROOKFINGERED JACK, clearly enjoying himself hugely, standing behind ROBIN.

ROBIN sounding troubled: *One coffee spoon. Real silver.*

A roar of laughter from the men. POLLY is furious and can scarcely contain herself.

POLLY trembling with anger: *Real silver?*

Close-up of ROBIN, looking crossly round while the merriment gets louder. As he does so, JACK pulls his fat wallet out of his pocket and waves it triumphantly in the air. This act of burglary is accompanied by a breathless hush.

The whole group of burglars is seen past POLLY. They are staring open-mouthed at ROBIN's wallet, but ROBIN himself is still confused and doesn't yet understand why his mood has changed so suddenly. Then he sees the wallet in JACK's hand and tries to snatch it from him, while the others push him aside, booing him. JACK counts out the contents of the wallet for POLLY to see.

POLLY's hand draws the money across the table towards her;

on either side, the heads of ROBIN and JACK. JACK is smirking contemptuously, while ROBIN is furious.

ROBIN snapping at JACK: *And what about your silver watch? How about the diamonds you got from that shop in Regent Street the day before yesterday?*

The laughter fades from JACK's face.

JACK hissing with fury: *Shut your trap!*

ROBIN grins; JACK pulls himself together.

JACK gasping: *And what did you hand over these last three Thursdays? You've been cheating the chief for years!* He turns to the others. *Isn't that so?*

Shot of the burglars.

A BURGLAR with a scornful laugh: *That's right!*

ROBIN leaps on him.

ROBIN fuming: *And how much did you put in your own pocket during the Thompson burglary?*

The other burglar looks embarrassed. JIMMY boos.

JIMMY: *Give it to him!*

WAT DREARY spins furiously round, making a threatening gesture towards JIMMY.

Close-up of JIMMY laughing.

WAT DREARY off: *You've got nothing to laugh about! Come and show us what you've put aside!*

JIMMY furiously: *Why me? Ned made more out of it than I did.*

The camera moves quickly to NED.

NED yelling fiercely: *That's not true at all! Jack's stowed away more money than all of us put together!*

The camera moves rapidly over the other burglars, who all start shouting threats at one another with angry faces.

BURGLARS: *Scoundrel! . . . Scoundrel yourself! . . . Cheat! . . . Crook! . . . Traitor! . . . etc.*

It comes to rest on JACK, who is pale and silent as he tries to retain his composure. Holding his head high in the face of the storm, he buttons up his coat and sticks his hands in his pockets.

Cut to POLLY. Her arms folded over the money, she looks warily at JACK and then her gaze wanders from one to the other as the uproar continues. She suddenly raps on the table with her pencil.

POLLY in a sharp voice, full of authority: *Silence!*

They fall silent. She continues in a vigorous tone that has a dangerous edge to it:

POLLY: *Bring out the money you've been embezzling!*

The burglars are seen past POLLY. They look grim and sullen and flash looks of hatred at each other.

POLLY: *Come on now! Are you going to do it? Otherwise I shall go straight to the Chief of Police and tomorrow* . . . Pointing at each of them in turn . . . *the whole rotten lot of you will have disappeared into the cells at the Old Bailey!*

The burglars, annoyed but beaten, turn sullenly round; some of them pull out their wallets and slam them angrily down on the table under POLLY's nose. A rapid series of close-ups shows:

A pair of hands lifting up one of the floorboards and pulling out a money-box.

A hand slitting open a straw mattress with a knife, whereupon a stream of banknotes gushes out.

From above, a hand turning the lining of a pocket inside out; a whole lot of pearl necklaces and other pieces of jewellery pour out onto the table-top. The camera moves higher and we see the top of the desk with an ever-growing heap of jewellery, coins, wallets and little iron money-boxes. POLLY's voice can be heard above the clinking of the coins and the jewellery.

POLLY off: *The burglary will not now take place. Why do we need to rob a bank when we've got enough capital here to open our own Bank?! Away from Soho and into the City!*

The mountain of coins and jewellery dissolves into the sign hanging outside a bank, which reads ' City Bank '. Dissolve.

*Scene 64. The directors' office in the bank.*
The room is furnished in a modern style and contains a desk, club-type fittings and a glass wall at the back giving onto the banking hall, where bank-clerks can be seen working feverishly. Beginning at the door, the camera tracks right through the room, past POLLY and JACK — absorbed in paperwork at their respective desks — and past three of the other burglars, now smartly dressed and smoking fat cigars as they recline in club armchairs. It finally holds for a moment on the glass wall

84

through which we can see the clerks slaving away. A bell has been ringing continuously during the fade-in. Now one of the clerks, a woman in her forties (the 'elderly spinster' type) stands up, walks up to the glass wall, knocks on the door, then opens it and comes into the directors' office.

FEMALE CLERK *very humbly: Did you want something, sir?*

JACK leans majestically back in his chair.

JACK: *Come and take dictation!*

The SECRETARY comes into shot and sits down at the type-writer near the desks. She has barely sat down when she suddenly leaps up again.

SECRETARY *bowing to* POLLY: *Good morning, Madam President!*

The camera tracks over to POLLY, who nods graciously and then becomes engrossed in her papers once again.

POLLY *in a detached tone, to the* SECRETARY: *Good morning, my dear.*

JACK has already begun to dictate and we hear the clattering of the typewriter.

JACK *dictating: First sales letter. In accordance with the honourable traditions of our institution etc, etc, we will endeavour to build up and increase the confidence of our customers . . .*

POLLY *correcting him: . . . clients . . .*

JACK: *. . . by the credit-worthiness of our bank in all transactions . . .*

The camera pans over to the three new members of the board, who are listening with broad grins on their faces, beaming contentedly. At that moment a voice bawls from the doorway:

VOICE off: *'Morning, boys!*

The men turn in horror and the camera pans to show WAT DREARY at the door. His clothes are not quite right somehow; he is not only unshaven and somewhat tipsy, but he is also wearing a long, brightly checked cravat with his tail-coat. The camera moves with him as he enters the room.

WAT DREARY *waving to* POLLY: *Pulled it off a treat, didn't we, ma'am!* He comes up to POLLY and holds out his hand. *Congratulations!*

Shot of POLLY, past WAT. She fails to notice his outstretched hand, stands up with great dignity and turns to the SECRETARY and dismisses her.

POLLY to the SECRETARY: *Thank you, my dear.*

She looks after the SECRETARY's retreating back, then turns her gaze on WAT, who has watched this little scene with a bewildered expression. He stares in amazament first at POLLY then at the disappearing figure of the SECRETARY, and finally at his colleagues in the background, hoping for a word of advice from them. POLLY's voice becomes very severe.

POLLY: *Do you really expect to fulfil the role of a director and member of the board in a suit like that, Mr Dreary? I really can't help laughing.*

The three 'members of the board' laugh, while WAT looks furiously round at them, utterly confused.

POLLY: *Silence! It's no laughing matter!*

The camera tracks back to show the members of the board standing stiffly to attention, while CROOKFINGERED JACK watches POLLY from his chair like a benevolent grandfather, nodding his approval.

POLLY: *In this new business of ours we can only use people of the highest calibre. Any fool can be a highwayman or a pickpocket. But what we're doing now is serious and you're incapable of rising to the situation, Mr Dreary! I'm going to pension you off!*

She sits down and writes something down on a piece of paper, shaking her head and muttering to herself as she does so.

POLLY: *A tail-coat with a green tie!*

She finishes writing and hands the piece of paper to JACK, who countersigns it. Then she hands it to WAT, addressing him in her former tone.

POLLY: *Go and report to the Chief of Police with this and get yourself locked up. You've earned the opportunity to retire!*

She claps him on the shoulder. He is totally bewildered and looks round to his colleagues for help, but they only shrug their shoulders. He staggers out of the room. The others watch him go.

POLLY breaking the silence: *It's eleven o'clock, Mr Mat of the Mint! Why aren't you over at the Stock Exchange?*

MAT snatches up a briefcase from where it is lying on a chair and darts through the door. POLLY sits down at her desk and gets back to work. Fade out.

*Scene 65. A street in London (as Scene 1).*

Fade in on part of a monument that was seen in the opening scene of the film. But whereas in the first scene it looked rather the worse for wear, and was dirty and inconspicuous, it is now being given a brilliant new coat of paint. There are people perched on various parts of the statue, washing down the great man's face and painting it over. The camera tracks back to show the whole of the statue and then more of the street. There are rugs hanging out of the windows, plus flags and garlands. Brushwood has been scattered on the roadway and workmen are feverishly working to get the decorations up, while the street is swarming with light-hearted throngs of people. A brass band can be heard in the distance. Policemen with white gloves and wearing dress uniforms are struggling vainly to control the traffic on this brilliantly sunny day. In a few hours the Coronation procession will be passing by. Our attention is immediately caught by a banner reading 'Long live our new Queen!' The camera tracks along the street and eventually holds on JENNY, who is caught up in the throng of passers-by, gaping at the preparations for the Coronation procession that are going on all round her. She looks up at the windows of the houses above her.

The camera tilts upwards from her point of view, over the rugs and garlands hanging down from the windows. As if by chance, it comes to rest on a window on the third floor of one of the houses. It is open and MACKIE and SUKY can be seen struggling to fix an enormous flag which is fluttering down almost as far as the first floor. MACKIE is in his shirtsleeves. Rapid dissolve to a shot of the two of them; they are totally engrossed in their work, like a pair of children absorbed in a game.

Then back to a close-up of JENNY's head, which is tilted back to look at them. Staring open-mouthed, she lets out an involuntary cry.

JENNY: *Mackie!*

The camera pulls rapidly back to show her pointing up at the window with one hand, the other hand to her mouth. She is staring at MACKIE oblivious of what is going on around her. People begin to collect round her, looking up also, and then a policeman pushes his way up to her. He too looks up at the window. Fade out.


Scene 66. PEACHUM'S *shop*.

The shop is full to bursting with beggars getting ready for the demonstration and painting placards and banners. There's a great deal of noise, what with the babble of voices from all sides, the distant sound of a brass band (which mixes in from the previous scene), the doorbell jangling repeatedly, the telephone ringing etc. The scene opens on a close-up of one of the banners with a hand painting it. It reads: ' I gave my eyes for the King!'

MRS PEACHUM off, at the top of her voice: *Come on! Come on!*

The camera tracks back slightly to show us the BLIND BEGGAR, who has pushed his glasses up onto the top of his head and is busy painting. MRS PEACHUM pushes her way through the assembled beggars, urging them on.

MRS PEACHUM: *If you're not willing to work you can't beg!* She walks over to the BLIND BEGGAR and examines his work with a critical eye. *You call yourself a blind man and you can't even form a ' K ' properly?*

The camera pans over the various different types of beggars as they work away. A renewed roll of drums is heard from the street.

A BEGGAR to one of his colleagues: *The Coronation procession!*

A moment's silence — all the beggars listen to what's going on outside. The camera tracks on and over to FILCH, who is feverishly taking orders behind the desk, using the telephone continuously.

FILCH: *Drury Lane branch? 350 men ready to go? Right you are!* . . . He hangs up, but the telephone rings again straight away. He snatches the receiver off. *Turnbridge branch?* . . . *Come on now, come on! Everything must be under way in one hour's time! How many banners? All right . . .!* He leaps up onto the desk. The camera tracks rapidly backwards . . . *Ladies and gentlemen! At this very moment 1,432 of our colleagues in eleven branches are working feverishly so as to be able to play a fitting part in our Queen's coronation.*[24] *In one hour from now we will assemble in front of Buckingham Palace and line the street. Departure of the poorest of*

*the poor half an hour later!*
The beggars let out a cheer, which mixes in with the cheering of the crowd in the next scene.

*Scene 67. The street (as Scene 1).*
The cheering of the crowd takes over from the cheering beggars in the previous scene. The police thrust the crowd to the side of the street, where they stand waving and shouting. Accompanied by the skirl of bagpipes, a platoon of Scots guards marches along the street, which is now clean and cleared of people. The sun is blazing down.

*Scene 68. BROWN's office.*
Several telephones on the desk are all jangling loudly at once. BROWN is half in his dress uniform and is clearly in a state of terrific excitement. He tears over to the desk, snatches up three telephones and speaks into all of them at once.
BROWN into the first telephone: *Yes! . . . No! . . . What a filthy trick! What? In Piccadilly as well? . . . Over 400 beggars? Into the second telephone: What? In front of Westminster as well? How many? More than 700? Arrest them! All of them! . . . Disperse them! . . . No, no, you fool! I can't scatter more than 10,000 beggars, on Coronation Day of all days! Into a third telephone: What? In front of Buckingham Palace . . .?*
He sinks exhausted into a chair. A POLICEMAN appears, looking agitated, walks over to BROWN and announces:
POLICEMAN to BROWN: *The Coronation procession is assembling!*
A roll of drums and a flourish of trumpets can be heard. SMITH appears, in a state of utter hysteria.
SMITH: *The beggars are setting off!*
The telephone rings. BROWN, who has completely lost his grip on things and doesn't know where to turn, puts his head in his hands. The telephone rings again. The camera tracks out as BROWN rushes round the office, completely at a loss, his head in his hands. SMITH walks over to the telephone and lifts the receiver. After a few moments he begins to speak.
SMITH in a strangled voice: *They've got him back!* Shouting aloud: *Mackie Messer has just been committed to prison!*
Everyone is paralysed for a moment. BROWN's eyes are popping

out of his head as he stares at SMITH blankly. Then he grasps what is happening, comes to a decision and, still only half-dressed, runs out of the door, pulling his coat on as he goes. SMITH and the policemen follow him.


*Scene 69. The prison,* MACKIE's *cell.*
PEACHUM is seen from the side, lying on the plank-bed, his legs drawn up and gazing at the ceiling. The lock rattles and the door is opened. At this sound PEACHUM quickly closes his eyes and begins to snore. BROWN comes into the picture and walks over to him.
BROWN: *Look here, Mr Peachum, you must leave!*
He shakes him, whereupon PEACHUM turns his back on him. BROWN sits down beside him, as if he were an invalid, and gives him a gentle but nervous shake, trying to convince him.
BROWN: *Pull yourself together, man! I'm revoking your arrest!*
PEACHUM stretches, yawns, raises himself on one arm and looks at BROWN sleepily as though he's just woken up from a deep sleep. BROWN's hopes begin to revive.
BROWN very quickly, to PEACHUM: *You must stop your demonstration!*
As PEACHUM makes no sign of having understood him, BROWN tries a new tack.
BROWN: *As one man to another — as one friend to another . . . You can't make difficulties for me today! I've fulfilled your requirements — Mackie Messer is under arrest! Look — they're bringing him in now!*
From PEACHUM's point of view, we see MACKIE approaching along the corridor outside the cell. He is literally buried under a welter of chains and the police escort is so big that it fills up the whole corridor. The policemen are all heavily armed. They line the corridor, their revolvers levelled at MACKIE. He gradually gets nearer to the cell.
Shot of PEACHUM, past BROWN; PEACHUM sits up on the plank-bed, pushing BROWN aside so as to get a better view. He looks at MACKIE with interest, a triumphant expression on his face. We see MACKIE in the doorway, then cut back to BROWN and PEACHUM. PEACHUM makes a disparaging gesture and sinks back on the plank-bed.

PEACHUM: *You'll only release him again!*

He rolls over on his side again, turning his back on BROWN. MACKIE stands in the doorway, waiting to come in. He tries to catch BROWN's eye, but BROWN takes no notice of him and instead rages up and down the cell, in terrible agitation. Then he walks over to PEACHUM once again.

BROWN to PEACHUM: *We won't release him! I give you my word of honour! He'll be hanged!*

MACKIE realizes he has no hope of awakening BROWN's interest, loses his assurance and almost faints. He is virtually shaking with fear.

BROWN to PEACHUM: *Well, then, get out of here.*

PEACHUM does not move but replies in a honeyed and affable tone:

PEACHUM: *I'm fine here.*

BROWN loses his last vestige of self-control and roars:

BROWN: *Police! Take him out!*

The POLICEMEN rush in, push MACKIE into the cell so as to get him out of their way, drag PEACHUM off the plank-bed and throw him out through the door and into the corridor, tossing him from one to the other. In the process, MACKIE gets whirled round on his own axis in the cell. BROWN disappears behind PEACHUM, snorting with rage. All the policemen follow him. The cell door slams shut. MACKIE is left speechless, scarcely grasping what's been going on, since it's all happened at such a speed. He stands in the middle of the cell, looks all round and then as the camera tracks slightly backwards we see a pair of heavily armed policemen patrolling the corridor on either side of the cell.

The camera tracks ahead of PEACHUM as he walks slowly along the corridor with BROWN beside him.

BROWN: *Here's a concrete proposal for you! You stop the demonstration — I hang Mackie — and the authorities will extend your licence for another three years!*

PEACHUM throws BROWN a searching sideways glance, but then keeps to his pose of indifference and walks on without saying a word. His steps get slower and slower. BROWN whispers to PEACHUM in an even more urgent tone:

BROWN: *And a hundred pounds in cash — for your trouble!*

PEACHUM, realizing that he has won, shows no sign of being interested, whereupon BROWN increases his offer.

BROWN: *A hundred and fifty!* Then as PEACHUM doesn't stir: *Two hundred!*

PEACHUM has almost come to a standstill, but still shows no interest, BROWN loses patience.

BROWN: *All right, then — no deal! Go and have your demonstration! !* He walks off, snorting with rage.

PEACHUM is at first bewildered, but then he pulls himself together. The camera closes in on his mouth as he yells after BROWN.

PEACHUM: *Hey, stop! Give me a chance to get a word in!* After a moment's pause: *Right! Two hundred! Done!*

Fade out.

*Scene 70. The directors' office at the bank.*

Fade in to a close-up of POLLY at her desk, speaking into the telephone. The last words from the previous scene mix into her first words.

POLLY: *. . . Five thousand? . . . Convert another three thousand into cash at once . . . Yes! By hook or by crook . . .!*

The camera tracks back a bit. POLLY hangs up and turns to the directors, amongst whom is JACK. They have been following the conversation with bated breath as they stand in a circle round POLLY.

POLLY: *Right, so we've rustled up the bail for the release of our chief.*

We hear the sound of the glass door being opened. They all turn towards it. The camera pans to show us a bank-clerk coming in with bundles of banknotes on a wooden tray. The camera tracks with him as he walks over to the desk, and lays the tray down on it. POLLY turns to JACK as the clerk begins to count out the packets of notes.

POLLY to JACK: *The money must be in the Chief of Police's hands within the hour, Mr Jack!*

JACK rushes eagerly forward and goes to pick up the money; the other two directors instinctively do the same. But POLLY, looking at them suspiciously, pushes their hands away with an equally instinctive gesture and bends right over the desk so that she can both protect the money and ring the bell.

A member of the bank's staff appears in the doorway. He is a very venerable-looking elderly man with a majestic beard; he is in uniform and holds his cap in his hand; a huge bank bag is attached to his belt. The camera tracks with him as he walks in a dignified manner over to the desk, opens the bag with a key and puts the money into it. The directors watch it disappear with unconcealed envy. While this is going on, POLLY speaks to him.

POLLY: *This is the money for the bail. Have the policemen we asked for arrived?*

ELDERLY EMPLOYEE: *Yes they have, Madam President.*

He hands over the key to POLLY, who shuts the bags and gives the key to JACK. Then he walks majestically out of shot towards the door.

At the door, he lets in the two policemen who have been waiting outside.

POLLY very vehemently, off: *These gentlemen from the police are personally responsible to me for the safe transport of the money!*

The policemen salute. The ELDERLY EMPLOYEE walks out first and they follow him stiffly. Then JACK comes into shot, nods towards POLLY and follows the others out.

We see POLLY standing beside the huge green-baize conference table. The seven main members of the board are either seated in the armchairs or about to sit down.

POLLY: *We will postpone our board-meeting so that my husband — I mean, our chief, can take part in the discussions.*


*Scene 71. The street outside the bank.*

We see an enclosed car (an old-fashioned model, 1900 vintage) parked in front of the door. Some policemen ward off curious passers-by who are trying to form a crowd. The ELDERLY EMPLOYEE comes out of the bank, followed by the policemen and JACK, and gets into the car. JACK and the policemen get in after him, one of the policemen sitting beside the driver. The car drives off.


*Scene 72. The Old Bailey, MACKIE's cell.*

In the cell, MACKIE is wandering round and round like a caged

93

lion, half-crazy with fear.

MACKIE murmuring to himself: . . . *They're going to hang me . . .
they're going to hang me . . . they're going to hang me!*

There is a distant sound of hammering on wood. MACKIE
starts, walks over to the bars and listens anxiously. The bang-
ing gets more eerie and more hollow. He stares wildly into
space and then a vision appears before his eyes . . .

Sinister-looking torturers are busy constructing a gallows . . .
MACKIE stuffs his fingers into his ears and rushes backwards
into a distant corner of the cell, his eyes glued to the vision.
The vision continues, accompanied by a distant roll of
drums . . .

MACKIE is no longer chained but wearing a condemned per-
son's shift, his neck bare. Two torturers lead him between a
double rank of policemen, all heavily armed and drumming
away. The drumming gets louder . . .

MACKIE covers his face with his hands and escapes to another
corner of the cell, where he clings onto the bars. The drumming
stops and instead we hear a bell tolling in the distance. It
sounds like the sort of bell that is tolled when a condemned
man is about to be executed. As he gazes through the bars,
MACKIE sees a different vision . . .

A huge pair of gallows: MACKIE is being dragged up the
steps. The vision disappears . . .

MACKIE collapses onto the floor of the cell and screams.

*Scene 73. The street scene (as Scene 1).*

The Coronation festivities have reached their climax; the
crowds are roaring, enjoying themselves hugely. The police can
scarcely keep them off the road. They are all laughing and
looking in the same direction — the Coronation procession will
soon be coming. A band is playing somewhere.

We see the car with MACKIE's bail inching its way through
the throngs of people. As it is on the point of turning into the
street a POLICEMAN stretches out his arm to prevent it going
any further. JACK opens the door and perches on the running-
board to peer ahead.

*Scene 74. The Old Bailey, MACKIE's cell.*

Behind the bars, MACKIE picks himself up from the floor, struggling to his feet as though he has just come round from a dead faint. Still on his knees, he sings 'A Cry from the Grave' (a shortened version, possibly combined with 'The Epitaph'). He rises to his feet and continues singing with his face pressed against the bars. Fade out.

*Scene 75. Outside* PEACHUM'S *shop.*
A vast throng of beggars are gathering in preparation for their march. Signboards, placards and banners rear up above their heads. There is total silence as they form ranks.
Seen past the front rank of beggars, PEACHUM approaches along the street. At first a tiny figure, he gets larger and larger and while he is still some way away he starts signalling and calling out:
PEACHUM: *Call off the demonstration! . . . Call it off! Call it off!*
At first they can't make out what he's saying, but eventually he comes up to them, breathless, bedraggled and pouring with sweat. Since the beggars merely look at him, not reacting to his shouts at all, he furiously pushes back the first two, who are carrying a large banner.
PEACHUM screaming: *Take it all back. The demonstration is cancelled.*
He tries to tear the banner from their hands. A shrill whistle is heard from behind.
Shot of the assembling crowd of beggars from in front, with PEACHUM in the foreground. The ones at the back push their way forwards, all whistling and yelling, waving their hands and brandishing their crutches. FILCH rides to the front of the column on a high old-fashioned bike and shouts:
FILCH: *Forward march!*
The front ranks begin to move. PEACHUM is very nearly trampled underfoot. He leaps out of the way and rushes over to FILCH.
We see FILCH on the bike with the furious figure of PEACHUM beside him, while behind them the crowd of beggars begins to march.
PEACHUM clutching at FILCH: *Back, I say! I'm in charge here!*

He tries to pull FILCH off his bike. FILCH struggles with him, the beggars pull PEACHUM off as they march past; there's momentary confusion, during which PEACHUM gets thrashed and FILCH rides on, the main body of the beggars behind him.

*Scene 76. Inside* PEACHUM's *shop.*
The open doorway is seen from inside the shop. There is a frightful noise coming from the street. MRS PEACHUM rushes towards the door and as the column marches past, PEACHUM retreats backwards into the shop and tries to shut the door, helped by MRS PEACHUM. But some of the beggars break in and give him a good thrashing, smashing the glass door in the process. More and more of them push their way in from the street. The camera tracks out to show the roaring throng of beggars tearing the shop apart.

*Scene 77. A dark, narrow street.*
Seen from a high angle, the procession of beggars march slowly and silently along, More and more people, the very images of poverty, come out of every nook and cranny, round every street corner. But these are figures of genuine wretchedness, among them haggard women holding small children by the hand. They join the beggars, so that the well organised procession soon breaks up into a jumbled mass of people shuffling slowly forwards.

*Scene 78. Inside* PEACHUM's *shop.*
We look down from the staircase above MRS PEACHUM as she runs down with a jug of water and over to the battered and unconscious figure of her husband. She tries to revive him and he slowly comes round and looks about him.
The camera pans from his point of view, showing the devastation in the shop and then, through the shattered door in the street, the legs and artificial limbs of the beggars. Fade out.

*Scene 79.* BROWN's *office in the Old Bailey.*
Close-up of some bundles of banknotes lying on BROWN's desk. The camera tracks out to show us BROWN himself on one side of the table and in front of him the ELDERLY BANK

EMPLOYEE, who is still taking bundles of notes out of his bag, with JACK standing beside him. The two policemen who escorted them stand stiffly behind them. BROWN sits down, takes a printed form and begins to write something.

The form is seen in close-up as BROWN puts his signature to it. We can make out only the bottom half of the form, the last words of which read '. . . is to be released at once '. After signing it, BROWN's hand takes a large round rubber stamp and presses it down on the form, then puts the stamp back, allowing us to read the words ' London's Chief of Police '. The image fades, so that we can see nothing but the circular inscription on the stamp, then this too dissolves into the next shot.

*Scene 80. The street outside the prison.*
Close-up of the circular inscription ' London's Chief of Police ' over the door of the prison. The camera tracks back to show us the door and a crowd of people besieging it. The police are holding the crowd back so that a passage is left clear from the door to the car from the bank, which is parked outside. Some photographers push their way to the front of the crowd, aiming their cameras at the door.

*Scene 81. BROWN's office in the Old Bailey.*
BROWN is seated at the desk on which he has stacked up the piles of notes. He walks over to the window and looks out into the street as distant cheers are heard from outside.

*Scene 82. The street outside the prison.*
The street is seen from BROWN's window, with the waiting crowd being held back by police. In front are the car and the ring of photographers, still with their cameras pointing at the door, from which MACKIE now emerges, triumphant and wreathed in smiles. He pauses on the top step and the ring of photographers closes in on him. He waves affably in all directions, while the crowd cheer in the background. He walks over to the car and climbs in. JACK climbs in and sits down behind him, while the ELDERLY BANK EMPLOYEE, his bag now empty, gets in beside the chauffeur. The car drives off. Fade out.

97

## Scene 83. A dark, narrow street.

Fade in to a high shot looking down onto the street. The throng of wretched humanity pours through, disappearing beneath the camera. The crowd entirely fills the street, in total disorder, the beggars disappearing in the welter of genuine poverty and misery. Distant cheers can be heard from the direction in which the crowd is marching.

## Scene 84. The street scene (as Scene 1).

The cheers continue: the festivities are at their height in a blaze of sunshine and merriment. In the foreground, the crowds wait lining the street. Beyond them at the next inter-section, the front of the Coronation procession is just turning the corner into the street and gradually getting nearer.

The procession is now seen in the foreground, beyond it the cheering crowds and a side street along which the throng of beggars, real and fake, are approaching. They turn into the main road. The cheering crowds and the policemen scatter, as the paupers surge forward and line the street in their place. More and more of them pour out of the sidestreet, swelling the waiting ranks.

Shot of the Coronation procession. In the foreground, the beggars stand waving their arms and artificial limbs threaten-ingly and raising high their banners. A magnificent gilded Baroque calèche surrounded by heralds and pages breaks into a hurried trot; the slow and ceremonial pace observed hitherto is thrown to the winds and pages and maids of honour start to run like hunted animals. A chorus of threatening shouts begins to arise from the beggars, leading us into the next scene.

## Scene 85. The directors' office in POLLY's bank.

The beggars' chorus continues, faintly at first, but rapidly getting louder. MACKIE is addressing the members of the board, who are assembled round the green-baize table in the foreground. POLLY is seated beside him and looks up at him lovingly as he talks. MACKIE suddenly stops in mid-sentence, his mouth open, and turns nervously to the window. All the others gaze in the same direction, as the noise and singing rise to a threatening crescendo.

MACKIE in a commanding tone: *Let the shutters down!*
The rattle of the shutters being rolled down continues into the next scene.

Scene 86. *The main banking hall.*
The clerks have leapt onto their desks in panic. Beyond them we see the wide plate glass windows and large entrance doors. Various members of the bank's staff are feverishly letting down the shutters.
We see the shutter over the main entrance, now lowered to less than a man's height above the floor. The sweating and tattered figure of BROWN rushes into the hall beneath it, just before it finally crashes down to the ground.

Scene 87. *The directors' office.*
The directors and MACKIE are standing in a group as BROWN rushes in in the background, wild-eyed and out of breath. MACKIE hurries over to him and virtually catches him in his arms. JACK pushes up an easy chair and BROWN sinks exhausted into it. The noise and singing in the street are ebbing away.
Close on BROWN as he seizes MACKIE's hand and whispers to him in an agitated and stricken tone:
BROWN: *The Coronation procession is ruined! I'm done for! . . . I shall have to resign! Oh Mack, I have been sacrificed on the altar of our friendship!*
MACKIE calming him down: *Chin up, old chap!*
JACK brings a glass of whisky to revive him.
MACKIE: *Drown your sorrows in this whisky! . . .* BROWN drinks it down and pulls himself together . . . *It's mutual, after all.*
MACKIE turns to his colleagues and the camera tracks slightly back to show them standing round.
MACKIE: *There's a lesson for you!* To BROWN: *There's no reason why a retired Chief of Police shouldn't make an excellent bank director!*
BROWN shakes MACKIE by the hand, beaming and breathing a sigh of relief. POLLY walks over to BROWN and addresses him in a solemn and businesslike tone.
POLLY: *What sort of stake can you put in?*
BROWN looks perplexed, but then a thought strikes him.

BROWN triumphantly: *I managed to rescue the bail money!*
He pulls bundles of banknotes out of all his pockets and lays them on the table. MACKIE and BROWN embrace each other, exactly as they did in the wedding scene, and in the photograph of the two of them in uniform. They begin to sing ' The Song of the Heavy Cannon ', with the burglars joining in the chorus.

*Scene 88. The street in front of the bank.*
The shutters are down. In the far distance we can see the tail end of the throng of beggars turning the corner as their singing fades softly away into the distance. PEACHUM, now scarcely recognizable, drags himself painfully along the street.
He walks past the bank, a broken man, leaning heavily on his stick, and the chorus of ' The Song of the Heavy Cannon ' swells out from behind the lowered shutters.
We see him from behind as he stumbles on. The camera is stationary and he grows smaller and smaller until he finally disappears into the mist. Fade out.

# NOTES

By comparison with the script published here, the final version of *The Threepenny Opera* is considerably condensed and reconstructed in a number of important ways. The dialogue, while following the sense of that given in the script, is often condensed almost to silent screen standards, while many scenes are cut or transposed. Significant divergences, both in structure and dialogue, are indicated in the following notes. It should be noted that the first half of the film follows the script fairly closely, and it may be assumed that scenes are included unless they are mentioned as being cut. From *Scene 48* onwards, the film diverges substantially from the script, and the only scenes included are those mentioned in the notes.

*Scene 1*
[1] In the film, as MACKIE grabs the cane by the handle, it comes apart and we see that it is a sword-stick with a long blade in it.

*Scene 2*
[2] In the film, our first view of MACKIE in this scene is as he comes round a corner between two spectators. The incident with the man with the top hat is omitted. During the initial action, the first three verses of 'The Ballad of Mackie Messer' are sung as follows:

> *Now the shark he has his teeth*
> *And he wears them in his face.*
> *Mackie Messer has a knife but*
> *Wears it in a discreet place*
>
> *On a lovely, sunny Sunday*
> *A man lies dead upon the shore.*
> *Another man strolls round the corner,*
> *Mackie Messer strikes once more.*
>
> *And Schul Mayer still is missing*
> *And many other fine rich men.*
> *Mackie Messer has their money*
> *But evidence is rather thin.*

[3] The next two verses of the song now follow:

101

*When they found poor Jenny Towler*
*With a knife stuck in her breast,*
*On the quay walked Mackie Messer*
*As innocent as all the rest.*

*Seven children and an old man*
*Burned alive in our Soho —*
*In the crowd is Mackie Messer,*
*He's not asked and does not know.*

[4] At this point, instead of showing us the girls with their liquorice sticks, the camera tracks away from the scene, showing the two women with MACKIE in pursuit. The STREET-SINGER delivers the final verse off-screen:

*And the widow, under age*
*The one whose name we know so well*
*Raped one night as she lay sleeping . . .*

Camera tracks ahead of MACKIE, smiling.

*. . . Mackie, how much could you tell?*

We resume on the SINGER as he repeats the last two lines of the song.
[5] Before *Scene 3*, the film shows the two women coming up the street and stopping in front of a shop with a sign saying MILLINERS. There is a wedding dress in the window and as POLLY gazes at it thoughtfully, she notices the reflection of MACKIE, who has come up behind her. She turns and MACKIE leans hungrily over POLLY, who is dragged unwillingly away by her mother.

*Scene 3*
[6] The exchange with WAT DREARY does not take place at this point. Instead, MACKIE sees JENNY approaching, and tells the doorman not to let her in.
[7] Once inside the inn, MACKIE tells one of his henchmen to go and deal with JENNY. The henchman goes outside and blocks JENNY's path as she tries to go in.

*Scene 4*
[8] The film first shows them arriving at a table in a corner of the bar. MACKIE stands menacingly over two characters seated at the table, who nervously raise their hats and vacate their places. (*Still*).
[9] Meanwhile, outside, JENNY is screaming at the doorman: *He's in there with a woman, isn't he?* The henchman restrains her bodily.
[10] In the film, this scene has even more point, since it is JACK's girl, not his whisky, from which he is torn away to dance with MRS PEACHUM.
[11] MACKIE stays at the table with POLLY and they gaze into one another's eyes. He silently asks her to marry him and she nods.

[12] Apart from the comment on JACK's abilities as a dancer to MRS PEACHUM, these are the first words which MACKIE is heard to utter in the bar scene. There then follows a condensed version of MACKIE's instructions for the wedding, which the man addressed passes on to the other burglars. MACKIE finally disappears upstairs with POLLY, leaving a written invitation to be delivered to TIGER BROWN, which the horrified burglars pass from hand to hand. The final dialogue between JACK and MRS PEACHUM is omitted.

## Scenes 5 to 9
The scenes involving the burglars are much condensed in the film. The episode with the double bed is omitted, and the serenade is displaced to a later point. The deaf-mute BEGGAR is also omitted, both from the scene with the clock *(Scene 9)* and from the scene in BROWN's office which follows.

## Scene 10
[13] In the film, MAT OF THE MINT is brought in as BROWN is berating his men: they have caught a thief ' red-handed '. BROWN turns on MAT and gives him dire warnings of the treatment he can expect, but is cut off in mid-flow by the sight of MACKIE's invitation, which is fastened inside the crown of MAT's hat so that only BROWN can see it. BROWN nervously orders the policemen out. *(Still)*.

## Scene 11
After the episode with NED and the armchair *(Still)*, the film moves straight on to *Scene 17*.

## Scene 17
In the film, the scene of the marriage, and MACKIE's headquarters, is a large warehouse beside the river, and not the stables of the Duke of Devonshire. All references to the place in the film are therefore to the ' warehouse ' rather than the ' stable '. At the beginning of this scene, the two burglars first appear through a trapdoor in the floor, leading from a lower storey of the warehouse. *(Still)*.

## Scene 18
The following scenes of the waggons approaching the stable are omitted. Instead a ramp is let down from the upper floor of the warehouse and the burglars, who have been waiting outside, swarm in with their stolen goods. At this point the serenade *(Scene 8)* is inserted, but takes place on a boat moored to the quayside by the river. POLLY appears in her

wedding dress, and the following dialogue takes place:

MACKIE: *Can you see the moon over Soho?*
POLLY: *I see it, dearest . . . Can you feel my heart beating, beloved?*
MACKIE: *I feel it, beloved.*
POLLY: *Where you are, there will I be too.*
MACKIE: *And where you are, I'll be at your side.* He begins to sing:
> *We have no licence from the registrar*
> *And no nice flowers on the high altar.*
> *Your wedding dress comes from somewhere afar*
> *And no myrtle crown for your hair.*
> *The platter from off which you now eat your bread,*
> *Don't look at it, cast it down.*
> *Love endures or fades away*
> *Either here or elsewhere, my own.*

He helps POLLY off the boat onto the quay and they walk away into the distance. (*Still*).
The scenes of the preparations in the warehouse then follow.

### Scene 22

The coachman is, of course, omitted, since in the film, MACKIE and POLLY are coming from the boat moored at the quayside.

### Scene 25

The comments from the various burglars are omitted in the film, and after a brief chorus of congratulations, MACKIE begins his tour of inspection; one of the burglars carries POLLY's train. At the end, POLLY comments:

POLLY: *How lovely! All stolen, Mackie?*
MACKIE: *Of course.*
POLLY: *A pity we've no home for these lovely things.*
[14] At this point, MACKIE instructs NED to escort the VICAR from the warehouse with the words: *The district is none too safe.* However, as soon as they get outside the terrified VICAR runs away.
[15] One of the burglars responds by standing on his hands on the table, juggling with some plates etc, but gets a very frosty reception.
[16] The song which POLLY sings is not ' Pirate Jenny ' but the following:
> *Once I believed, when innocent I was —*
> *And I really was once, same as you —*
> *Perhaps someone will soon be my suitor,*
> *Then I must know what to do.*
> *And if he's rich and if he's nice,*
> *And if his collar's white as snow,*

And if he knows how to treat a lady,
Then the answer's No.

Then you stick your nose up in the air
And let your righteous virtue glow.
Sure the moon is brighter than before,
Sure the boat goes gliding from the shore,
But that's as far as you should go.
Yes, but you don't simply lay yourself down,
Yes, be as cold and heartless as you know,
Yes, there's so much that can happen,
Yes, there's just one answer, No!

The first was a man who came from Kent,
He was all that a man should be.
The second had three ships in the harbour,
The third was mad about me.
And they had money, and they were nice,
And their collars were as white as snow,
And they knew how to treat a lady —
To them I answered No!

Then I stuck my nose up in the air
And I let my righteous virtue glow.
Sure the moon was brighter than before,
Sure the boat went gliding from the shore,
But that's as far as I would go.
Yes, but you don't simply lay yourself down,
Yes, be as cold and heartless as you know,
Yes, there's so much that can happen,
Yes, there's just one answer, No! . . . No?

Then came another who didn't try to beg
One day when the sky was blue.
He hung his hat on the peg in my room,
Then I didn't know what to do.
He had no money, he wasn't nice,
His collar was never white as snow.
He didn't know how to treat a lady,
Yet I couldn't say to him No.

I couldn't stick my nose up in the air,
And forgot my virtue's glow.

*Oh the moon was brighter than before,*
*But the boat never glided from the shore,*
*Then I had no choice and so . . .*
*Yes, then you must simply lay yourself down,*
*Yes, then you can't be cold and heartless, you know.*
*Yes, there's so much that did happen.*
*Yes, I couldn't hope to answer No.*

The song is accompanied by alternating shots of POLLY, MACKIE and the listening burglars. At the end of the song the burglars applaud enthusiastically and one of them says: *I like the words, very nice.* To which MACKIE replies scornfully: *Nice! It's not nice, it's art, you fool!* To POLLY: *Wonderful! Too good for this trash.*
[17] *Still.*

## Scene 26
This scene is omitted from the film, and so is all reference to the fight between the three beggars in the later scenes in PEACHUM's shop.

## Scene 28
[18] PEACHUM's song is omitted from the film.

*Scene 29* is displaced to within *Scene 30.*

## Scene 30
[19] *Still.*
[20] At this point we move to POLLY's bedroom, and PEACHUM's discovery of her absence takes place on-screen. POLLY then arrives immediately, the robbery of the safe by MACKIE's gang being omitted. The argument with her parents in *Scene 32* takes place in POLLY's bedroom (*Still*), and her song in *Scene 33* is omitted.

## Scene 34
[21] The film at this point includes a scene in TIGER BROWN's office, in which PEACHUM threatens trouble at the forthcoming Coronation if BROWN does not arrest MACKIE and have him hanged. The dialogue is adapted from that used in *Scene 61* of the script.

## Scene 35
The STREET-SINGER's song, in the film, runs as follows:
*Man lives through his head,*
*A head fit for a mouse.*
*Just test it out, your little head,*
*It wouldn't feed a louse.*

For our life in this world,
Man is very much too dim.
Never does he notice
Everyone deceiving him.

Yes, make yourself a plan,
Yes, be a shining light.
Then make yourself a second plan
And both your plans will fight.

For our life in this world,
Man is not corrupt enough.
Yet his aspirations
Provide a noble touch.

Yes, just you chase your luck,
But don't you run too fast,
Since all who push their luck too much
Find that they come in last.

For our life in this world
Man assumes too much.
So all his aspirations
Are self-deceptive gush.

## Scene 36
MACKIE MESSER'S headquarters, as seen in the film (*Still*), is described by Paul Rotha in *Celluloid* (see Appendix). The conversation between MACKIE and POLLY in this scene is greatly condensed, but follows the sense of that in the script.

## Scene 38
[22] In the film, POLLY slaps MAT'S face with the comment: *Nothing personal, of course.*

## Scenes 39 and 40
These are omitted in the film, and *Scene 48* — JENNY'S exchange with MRS PEACHUM (*Still*) — takes place before MACKIE'S entry into the brothel.

## Scene 47
[23] *Still.*
The conversation between MACKIE and JENNY is somewhat condensed in

the film. MACKIE then turns his attention to the other girls and JENNY walks over to the window and signals to the waiting policemen. Standing in front of the window, she then begins to sing ' The Ballad of the Ship with Fifty Cannon ' (and not the ' Tango Ballad '). The song runs as follows:

> Today I wash glasses and make up the beds
> Servant to one and all, sir.
> Give me a penny and I thank you well
> For I live in rags in a dirty hotel,
> But you don't know who I am, sirs.
>
> But one night soon there'll be screaming by the harbour
> And then they'll be in terror all the while.
> Then I'll be smiling to my glasses
> And they'll ask, Why should she smile?
>
> And a ship with eight great sails
> And with fifty fine cannon
> Will tie up at the quay.
>
> Dear sirs, it'll take the smile off your faces
> When the walls come tumbling in.
> The town will be flattened right to the ground,
> Just this dirty hotel left safe and sound
> And you'll wonder who lives within.

At this point MACKIE comes up, having left the other girls, and listens intently to JENNY's song.

> But in the night there'll be shrieks round this hotel
> And they'll wonder why it should be standing free,
> And they'll see me step outside in the morning
> And they'll be saying, Who is she?
> And they'll be saying, Who is she?
>
> And a ship with eight great sails
> And with fifty fine cannon
> Will run up her flag.
>
> At mid-day hundreds will swarm ashore
> Searching every street and hill,
> Rounding up survivors who'll be shivering with fear,
> Wrapping them in chains and bringing them all here,
> And they'll ask me, Which shall we kill?
> And they'll ask me, Which shall we kill?

> At this very hour there'll fall a hush on the harbour
> And they'll ask me, Who shall die?
> And then you'll hear me order firmly, All.
> When the heads fall I'll cry, Hoppla!
>
> And a ship with eight great sails
> And with fifty fine cannon
> Will then sail off with me.

Instead of dancing MACKIE into the arms of the waiting police, JENNY now relents. She tells him he has been betrayed and hides him behind a curtain as the police search the brothel. JENNY diverts the police with the words: *He went through the window*, and MACKIE then walks nonchalantly out onto the roof.

From this point on, the sequence of events in the film departs substantially from that in the script, and the following notes therefore itemise each scene as it occurs.

*Scenes 48 and 49*
These are omitted, and instead MACKIE, having made good his escape, falls in with another tart in the street and disappears into her lodging with her as the police search for him outside. This episode is clearly suggested by *Scene 57* in the script.

MRS PEACHUM meanwhile returns to inform PEACHUM that MACKIE has escaped:
MRS PEACHUM: *He escaped. The girl helped him.*
PEACHUM: *Tiger Brown's the girl's name. Now for the Coronation . . .*

MACKIE emerges again from the tart's lodging, takes leave of her and walks straight into the arms of the waiting police.

We now see the STREET-SINGER, who addresses the camera as follows:
STREET-SINGER: *Ladies and gentlemen, you have seen Mackie's flippancy and boldness . . . Now see how a shrewd, loving wife alters events in a way you can't predict.*

The film then moves to a version of *Scene 64*, in which POLLY addresses the directors of the newly instituted bank, then we return to *Scene 50*.

*Scene 50*
This scene is substantially cut in the film. It opens with an exchange between SMITH and BROWN (this is SMITH's first appearance in the film):

BROWN: *Give him everything he asks for!*
SMITH: *Cigarettes too?*
BROWN: *No — here, give him a cigar.* He hands SMITH some cigars from his pocket.
We then move to the conversation about the handcuffs between SMITH and MACKIE, during which MACKIE is horrified to hear the sound of an execution taking place off-screen.

*Scenes 51 and 52*
The character of LUCY does not appear in the film at all, and it is JENNY who in fact comes and visits MACKIE in prison (*Stills*), and engineers his escape by seducing SMITH. Moreover, this episode is displaced to a later point and the film moves directly from *Scene 50* to *Scene 66* — the preparations for the procession of beggars.

*Scene 66*
In this scene it is not FILCH but PEACHUM who gets up on the desk and addresses the beggars, who are alarmed at the sound of the royal guard off-screen.
[24] In the film PEACHUM's speech continues: *You can participate in this glamorous event. You'd all be dead but for my fund-raising schemes. I discovered that the rich can't face the misery they make. They've got cold hearts but weak nerves . . . No consideration for their nerves today! We'll tear their nerves with all our power. Our rags won't cover our wounds . . . Don't be afraid, gentlemen, the Queen won't tolerate bayonets against cripples.*
At this point MRS PEACHUM rushes in with the news that MACKIE has been arrested, and PEACHUM tries to stop the procession, which has now got under way. However, he is swept aside by the silently marching beggars. This sequence matches that given in *Scenes 75* and *76* of the script, but FILCH's leadership of the mob is not in evidence.

We then return to the STREET-SINGER, who gives his acid comment on the proceedings:
STREET-SINGER:
> *Yes, make yourself a plan,*
> *Yes, be a shining light,*
> *Then make yourself a second plan*
> *And both your plans will fight.*
> *For our life in this world*
> *Man is not corrupt enough,*
> *Yet his aspirations*
> *Provide a noble touch.*

The film next moves to the bail scene *(Scene 70)*, then we return to PEACHUM being swept aside by the advancing tide of beggars. The episode in which PEACHUM visits BROWN at the Old Bailey and gets locked in MACKIE's cell is of course omitted from the film, which next moves to JENNY's visit to MACKIE in jail — an adaptation of *Scene 52*. SMITH is just bringing MACKIE his dinner, and JENNY persuades him to let her see MACKIE with the words: *I'll let you come and see me tonight . . .* SMITH opens the cell and goes in to give MACKIE his dinner. JENNY then folds him in an embrace at the bars and gestures to MACKIE, who sneaks out of the cell, locking the door behind him.

The film then returns to the procession of beggars as they encounter the police.

Meanwhile, BROWN is receiving the news of the demonstration in his office. This is an adaptation of *Scene 68* in the script — except that SMITH is not present (being locked in MACKIE's cell) and BROWN is of course under the impression that MACKIE is still in jail. In this scene, the BANK EMPLOYEE arrives with MACKIE's bail *(Scene 79* in the script). BROWN immediately phones the cells to order MACKIE's release, only to find that he has escaped.

Amid the crowds waiting for the Coronation procession, MACKIE, on the run, encounters one of his gang in the street. The burglar informs MACKIE that he is now the managing director of a bank: *The City Bank . . . in Piccadilly*. MACKIE is highly approving and makes off towards the bank.

We now see the horde of beggars as it converges on the Coronation procession *(Scene 84* in the script). The beggars charge into the procession, and there is a dramatic confrontation as they come face to face with the open carriage in which the QUEEN is riding. Unable to bear the beggars' gaze, the QUEEN finally hides her face behind her fan, and the carriage moves on.

Now the mounted guards charge the beggars and disperse them, while BROWN — also in guard's uniform — watches in despair from his horse. *(Stills)*.

The film then moves to the bank, as *Scene 85*. First there is a reunion between MACKIE and POLLY, then one of the burglars announces the news that the Coronation has been ruined by thousands of beggars. The shutters are lowered.

Outside, BROWN rides up on his horse, dismounts and goes into the bank.

We see the procession of beggars sweeping past in silence.

BROWN then blunders into the bank, where everything is in darkness. Candles are brought, and the directors gather round (Scene 87 in the script). After BROWN has deposited the bail money, MACKIE and BROWN drink to friendship and reminisce over their times in the Indian Army — they break into ' The Song of the Heavy Cannon ', as follows:

MACKIE: *John was there and Jim was too*
BROWN: *And George was made a sergeant.*
MACKIE: *But the Army doesn't give tuppence for you*
BROWN: *As it sets its men a-marching.*

BOTH: *Soldiers depend on the heavy cannon*
 *From Cape to Couch Behar.*
BROWN: *If they should chance to meet,*
MACKIE: *In sunshine, snow or sleet,*
BROWN: *Another sort of race,*
MACKIE: *Dark or fair of face,*
BOTH: *They chop them up to make some beefsteak tartare.*

MACKIE: *Johnny thought whisky rather warm*
BROWN: *And Jimmy was short of blankets,*
MACKIE: *But Georgie took them by the arm*
BROWN: *Crying, The Army will always vanquish.*

BOTH: *Soldiers depend on the heavy cannon*
 *From Cape to Couch Behar.*
BROWN: *If they should chance to meet,*
MACKIE: *In sunshine, snow or sleet,*
BROWN: *Another sort of race,*
MACKIE: *Dark or fair of face,*
BOTH: *They chop them up to make some beefsteak tartare.*

MACKIE: *Johnny and Jimmy are both long dead*
BROWN: *And Georgie is broken and missing,*
MACKIE: *But blood is blood and always red*
BROWN: *And the Army's still recruiting.*

EVERYONE IN CHORUS:
 *Soldiers depend on the heavy cannon,*
 *From Cape to Couch Behar.*
 *If they should chance to meet*
 *In sunshine, snow or sleet*

> *Another sort of race,*
> *Dark or fair of face,*
> *They chop them up to make some beefsteak tartare.*

The ending of the film is radically different from the script, since PEACHUM now enters (instead of passing by the bank, a broken man, as in *Scene 88*). The following conversation takes place:

PEACHUM: *Poor Peachum and rich Mackie ought to join hands.*

MACKIE: *You're bankrupt, honest Mr Peachum. A poor devil like the rest.*

PEACHUM: *Today I've seen the power of the poor . . . Your money and my experience, a mighty business.*

He sits down and produces some contracts which he and MACKIE proceed to sign.

MACKIE: *Why do they need us, if they're so powerful?*

PEACHUM: *They don't know it, but it's we who need them!*

As they sign the contracts, the STREET-SINGER is heard over:

STREET-SINGER:

> *Gathered for the happy ending*
> *All crowd under the same hat.*
> *If good money is quite handy,*
> *Everything ends well for that.*
> *Hinz and Kunz fish muddy waters,*
> *Wish each other quickly dead,*
> *Yet in the end around the table*
> *They both share the poor man's bread.*

As he continues, we see the procession of beggars filing silently past in the street outside.

STREET-SINGER:

> *Therefore some live in the darkness*
> *And the others in the light,*
> *We see those who live in the daytime*
> *But not those who live in night.*